P A C I F I C
MAP OF

SARAH PALIN

AN AMERICAN STORY

★ A COLLECTOR'S VAULT ★

DAVE LIFTON

Sarah Palin
An American Story
A Collector's Vault

3101 Clairmont Road, Suite G, Atlanta GA 30329

Correspondence concerning this book may be directed to the publisher at the address above, attn: Sarah Palin Vault.

ISBN: 0794832768
Authored in the United States of America
Printed and assembled in China

This book was prepared for educational and informational purposes regarding the life and times of Sarah Palin. The publication includes material from a wide variety of sources and sociopolitical and historical materials. Whitman Publishing is not affiliated with or endorsed by any individuals, organizations, or entities referenced in this book. The reader will find commentary and analysis of the included materials, which assist historians in performing their own analysis and forming their own opinions. We hope this book is helpful in your study of the life and times of Sarah Palin.

Note: All removable documents and memorabilia in this book are replicas, not originals, and are for use exclusively in connection with this publication and are not for separate use or resale.

CONTENTS

Prologue

COUNTRY FIRST

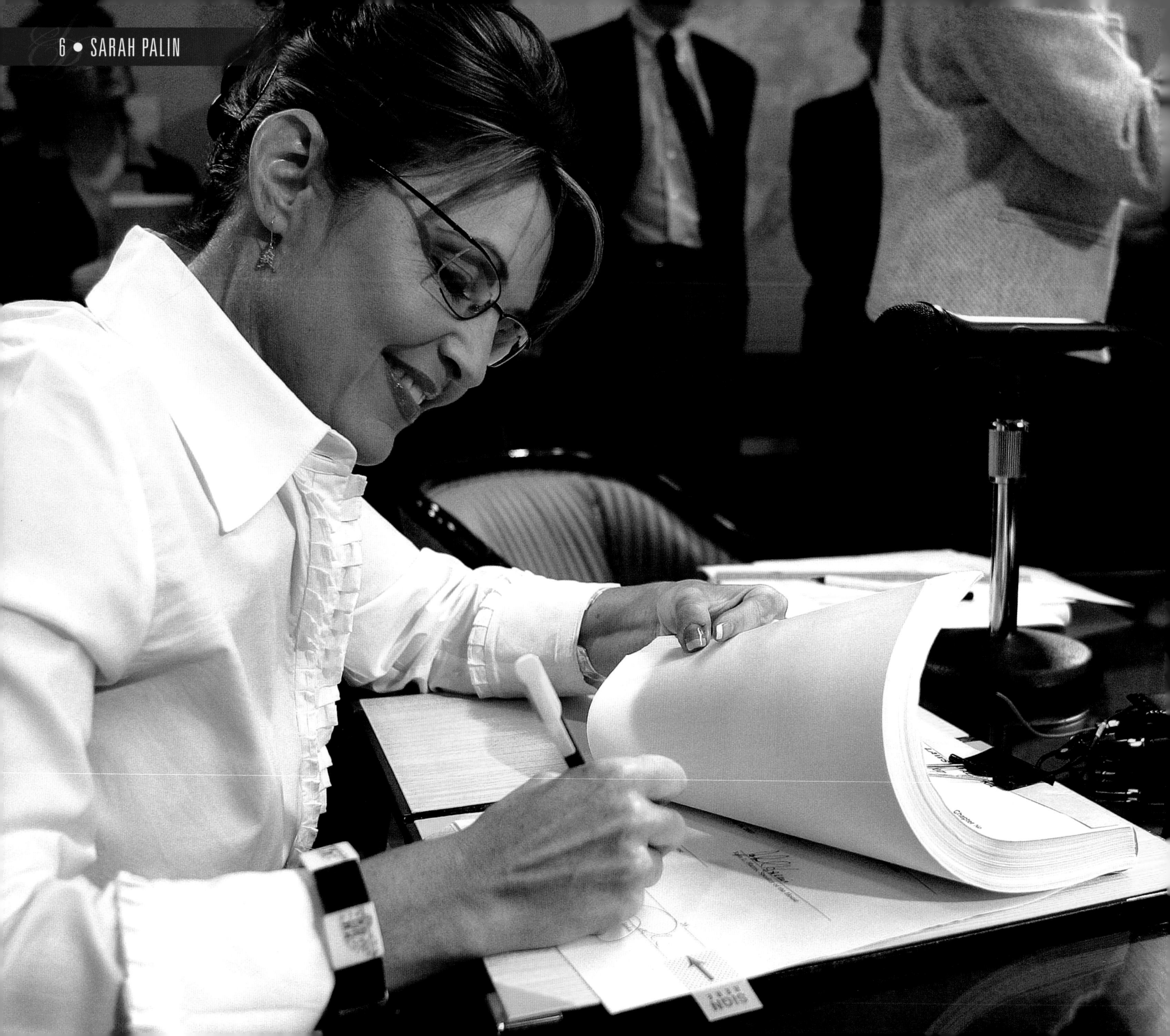

Few politicians in recent memory have drawn as much attention in a short period of time as Sarah Palin. Since she burst into the national spotlight in the summer of 2008, Palin's message has resonated with millions of Americans who share her values. With charisma and a folksy manner she has, almost singlehandedly, started a new political movement in this country.

Palin's rise from small-town Alaskan mayor to one of the leading voices in the conservative movement is a true American success story. Whether she is taking on Big Oil as governor or giving a rousing speech at a Tea Party rally, her belief in her convictions is unwavering. Along the way she has faced critics and personal hardship, but has persisted due to her family, faith, and abilities.

Yet for all that has been said and written about her, very little is still known about Sarah Palin. Her words and achievements have often been distorted by those seeking to promote their own agenda, but her record, as a politician and an activist, speaks for itself.

Whether she chooses to run for president in the future, or to remain politically active within the private sector, has yet to be determined. What is certain is that she will take on these challenges with the same dedication and seriousness of purpose that have been her hallmark.

Throughout her career, Sarah Palin has succeeded by bucking the system, defying expectations, and speaking her mind. In doing so, she has become one of the most fascinating and talked-about women of our time.

Alaska governor Sarah Palin signs a budget bill into law in Anchorage, Friday, June 29, 2007—cutting more than $250 million from the $1.8 billion capital budget the state legislature sent to her.

Chapter 1

From Idaho to Alaska

A view of the Parks Highway heading through Wasilla, Alaska. The date is Friday, August 29, 2008. Republican presidential candidate Senator John McCain has just chosen his vice-presidential running mate: Alaska's governor, Sarah Palin, a former mayor of Wasilla.

The Heath family's first home in Alaska was Skagway, a city on the Alaska Panhandle.

The woman the world knows as Sarah Palin was born Sarah Louise Heath on February 11, 1964, in Sandpoint, Idaho, to Charles "Chuck" and Sarah "Sally" Heath. A few months after her birth, her father accepted a teaching position in Skagway, Alaska, and the family moved to the 49th state, which had been admitted into the Union only five years earlier.

In 1969, the family—which included Sarah's older brother, Chuck Jr.; her older sister, Heather; and younger sister, Molly—moved into a duplex 15 miles outside Anchorage, the state's largest city. A few years later, the Heaths bought a house in a small, newly incorporated city in the Matanuska-Susitna (Mat-Su) Valley. That city—Wasilla—would eventually become world renowned through its most famous resident.

(Left) Alaska is well known for its wildlife, including its bears. "Dad would give us a quarter for being the first to spot a moose or a bear on our hour-long drives into Anchorage." (*Going Rogue,* page 20) Sarah credits her father for teaching her and her sisters to appreciate Alaska's pristine beauty and wildlife. Here, a mother brown bear guards her cubs on the banks of the Brooks River in Katmai National Park while other bears catch red salmon swimming up the river to spawn.

(Opposite page, right) Skagway first developed as the gateway port for gold miners drawn to the Yukon Gold Rush in the 1890s. The White Pass Railway began construction in 1898 to link Skagway to the inland mountain cities growing up around the miners—such as Bennett, British Columbia, and Carcross and White-horse, Yukon, Canada—and was completed in 1900, by which time the gold rush was already abating. After closing in 1982, the railway opened again thanks to a tourism boom from cruise ships; visitors are now able to retrace the route taken by miners more than a century ago as far as Carcross, a 67.5-mile trip taking six hours.

(Above) The Heath family's current home in Wasilla is adorned with hunting trophies. Here, Sarah's parents, Chuck and Sally Heath, watch as she is chosen by John McCain as his running mate and choice for vice president August 29, 2008.

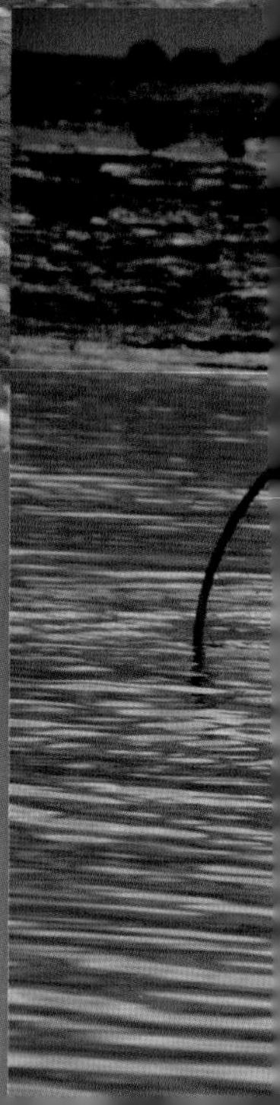

These scenes show some of the many sources of outdoor recreation in Alaska. *(Above right)* Children race through snow at the Eagle River Lions Park during the annual community Easter Egg Hunt in Eagle River, Alaska, on April 4, 2010. *(Above)* Aquatic recreation and cold-water safety courses are popular with children. Here, a rescue swimmer pops up in the middle of a group of third-graders in survival suits. *(Left)* Kayaking Alaska's rivers and other waterways is a popular pastime. Here, kayakers paddle around a southeast Alaska bay amid chunks of ice from nearby glaciers.

"In so many ways, Alaska is a playground. When Lower 48 parents tell their kids, 'Go play outside!' there may be limited options in suburban backyards. But Alaska kids grow up fishing the state's 3 million lakes in the summer and racing across them in the winter on snowmachines, kicking up rooster tails of snow." (*Going Rogue,* page 17)

(Above) Two snowmachines collide (without any subsequent injuries) during the Fur Rondy Snow Cross snowmachine race on February 25, 2006, in Anchorage. *(Left)* One of Alaska's most popular activities is fishing. Here, two Alaskans dipnet for red salmon in the Kenai River.

Located in the northwestern corner of North America, and isolated from the "Lower 48," the state of Alaska has a unique history. The name *Alaska* comes from *Alyeska,* which means "great land" in the language of the Aleuts, one of the native tribes who first arrived in the area approximately 10,000 years ago.

In the summer of 1741, Russians began exploring the islands and parts of the Alaska Peninsula. Eventually they began to settle in the area, first as fur traders, with Russian Orthodox missionaries coming later.

On March 30, 1867, Secretary of State William H. Seward signed a treaty with Russia, giving Alaska's 586,412 square miles to the United States for the price of $7.2 million, or 1.9 cents per acre. The treaty was ratified by the U.S. Senate less than two weeks later, and the official transfer of land took place on October 18, 1867. Every year, the anniversary of the transfer is celebrated as Alaska Day, a state holiday.

Historical Alaska: The "Great Land"

Toward the end of the 18th century, Spain, after learning of Russian involvement in Alaska, sent several expeditions there in their attempts to colonize the entire west coast of North America. But by 1819, they transferred their claims to the United States.

In 1778, Captain James Cook of Britain sailed to Alaska, becoming the first to make an accurate map of the entire North Pacific. Cook Inlet, on which Anchorage, Alaska's largest city, is located, is named in his honor. Canada-based Hudson's Bay Company was active there in the regional fur trade for many years.

By the mid-1800s, Russia's profitability in its Alaskan interests declined as a result of increased involvement by both the Americans and the British. Looking to prevent Alaska from falling into British hands following the Crimean War, the Russians offered the land to the United States.

(Right) Alexander II, czar of Russia, finalized the sale of Alaska to the United States. In this circa-1865 portrait, he wears the greatcoat and cap of the Imperial Horse-Guards Regiment.

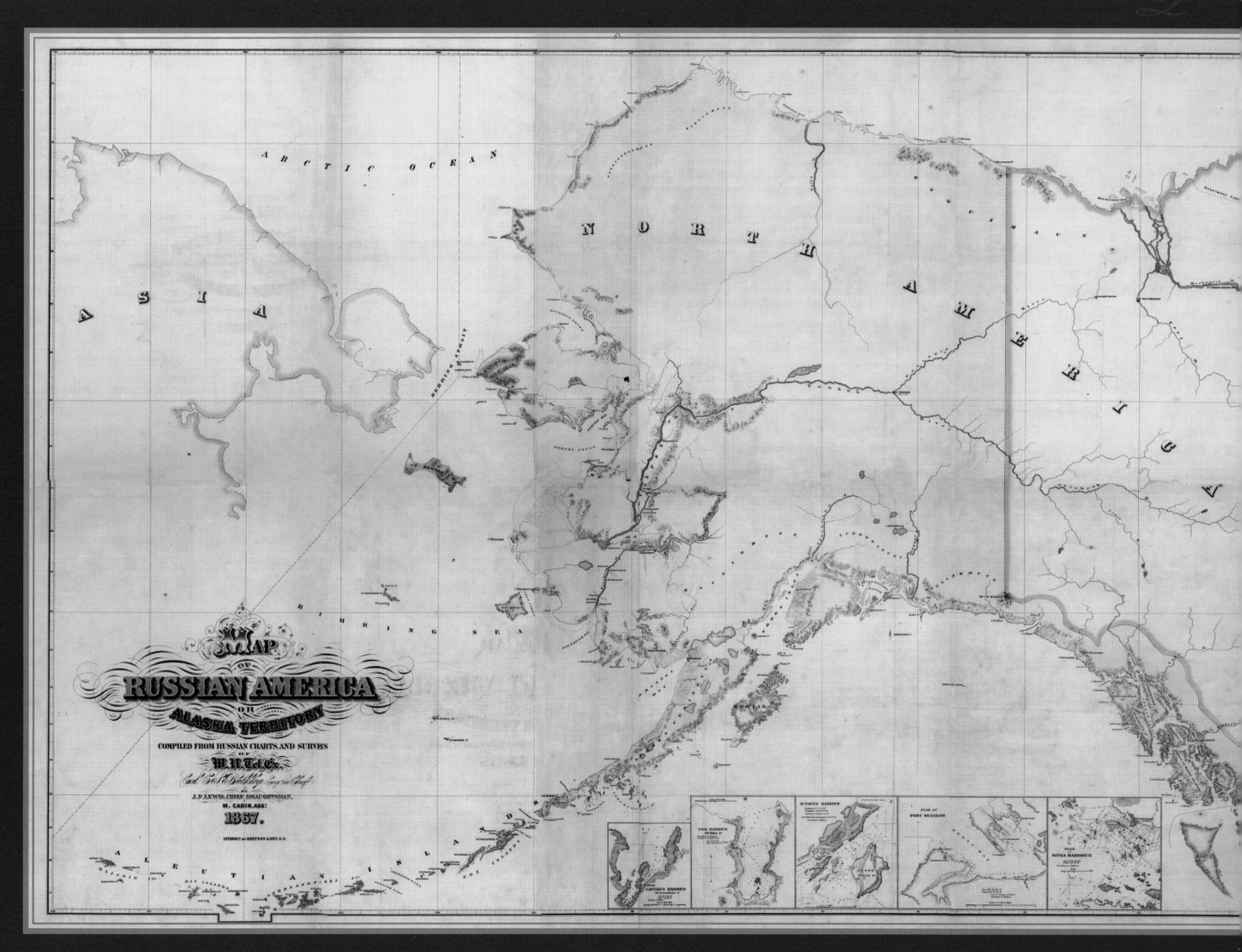

(Above) This map of Russian America was made in 1867, the year the United States purchased Alaska. By that time the region had been explored and settled by Russians for more than 100 years.

Nearly 30 years later, the Klondike Gold Rush began in Canada's Yukon Territories, and the existing trade routes in nearby Alaska benefited, as towns sprang up. The discovery of gold in Nome in 1899 led to even more development near the mines. In the first years of the 20th century, commercial fishing and canning became major industries in the District of Alaska.

Alaska officially became a territory in 1912. During World War II, the Japanese tried to invade the United States by occupying two of the Aleutian Islands. What should have been a quick battle turned into a 14-month struggle due to the weather conditions and terrain on the islands. The Aleutian Islands Campaign, as it was known, was won by the U.S. in August 1943.

(Above) Alaska has captured the American imagination for decades, as seen in these pieces of pop culture—valuable collectibles today. The 1952 Abbott and Costello lobby card was part of a small collection of photos and cards that sold for $107 in May 2010; the *Lulu and Tubby* comic book (from 1959, the year Alaska entered the Union) went for $215. In 2009, the 14 x 22–inch window card of Charlie Chaplin's 1925 classic *The Gold Rush,* set in Alaska's Klondike, was auctioned for more than $10,000.

The battle proved the strategic importance of Alaska due to its trade routes. Discovery of oil in the Swanson River on the Kenai Peninsula in July 1957 showed its economic benefits. A year later, President Dwight D. Eisenhower signed the Alaska Statehood Act, and, on January 3, 1959, Alaska became the 49th state admitted into the Union.

(Below) The *Alaska Galop,* copyright 1882, evoked the northern frontier by way of piano.

(In pocket) The United States purchased Alaska from Russia with this check for the sum of $7.2 million—less than 2¢ per acre. The check is made out to Edouard de Stoeckl, the Russian minister to the United States, who negotiated on behalf of the empire. (*also inside*) This Treaty of Cession was signed by Czar Alexander II, formally concluding the purchase agreement.

In 1968, more oil was discovered in Alaska, this time on the North Slope's Prudhoe Bay. It was determined that the best way to transport the oil was to construct an 800-mile pipeline connecting the North Slope with the port city of Valdez. But land acquisition, which involved negotiating with native tribes, and the act of building the pipeline through the frozen wilderness created challenges for the massive project.

Construction began in 1974, after an oil crisis the year before created a greater demand to reduce dependency on foreign oil. After a cost of $8 billion, the Trans-Alaskan Pipeline opened in 1977.

The pipeline brought billions of dollars into the state's coffers. But Alaska's history with oil production has not always been positive. On March 24, 1989, an oil tanker, the *Exxon Valdez,* hit Bligh Reef on Prince William Sound, spilling 11 million gallons of crude oil into 1,100 miles of water. The spill took years to clean up, but not before hundreds of thousands of animals were killed and considerable long-term damage to the ecosystem of Prince William Sound was done.

This 1920 photograph is entitled "Dog Sled Team Barking," or, alternately, "The Malamute Chorus." It shows a popular symbol of Alaskan life.

(Attached) Alaska's state quarter was one of 50 released by the U.S. Mint between 1999 and 2008, to celebrate the states that make up the Union. Traditionally, each governor was present for his or her state coin's official debut ceremony. Governor Palin's absence from the Alaska ceremony is understandable, though: just hours earlier, she had been named John McCain's vice-presidential running mate. Her lieutenant governor stepped in for the coin's official release.

THE MALAMUTE CHORUS C35

(Above) The Library of Congress notes that "Indian babies made popular subjects for commercial photographers, and Winter & Pond produced this image as a Christmas card. The child, wearing a cap covered with buttons, snuggles into a birchbark sling rigged with a rocking mechanism. The style of the cap appears Tlingit, but the infant's moccasins and the sling are probably of Athabaskan origin." The circa-1905 photograph was taken by Lloyd V. Winter and Percy E. Pond, who started their Juneau, Alaska, studio in 1893 and captured the faces and landscapes of southeastern Alaska into the 1940s. Its cardboard mount is marked "Alaska Slumberland."

President Dwight D. Eisenhower signed the Alaska Statehood Act, and, on January 3, 1959, Alaska became the 49th state admitted into the Union. "Ike" is seen here in his official White House portrait, and on a commemorative silver dollar issued by the U.S. Mint in 1990.

April 9, 1989: crude oil from the tanker *Exxon Valdez* swirls on the surface of Alaska's Prince William Sound. On June 15, 2009, Exxon Mobil Corp. was ordered by the 9th U.S. Circuit Court of Appeals to pay about $500 million in interest on punitive damages for the spill, nearly doubling the payout to Alaska Natives, fishermen, business owners, and others harmed by the disaster. "It took twenty years for Alaska to achieve victory," Sarah Palin wrote in *Going Rogue.* "When the *Exxon Valdez* hit Bligh Reef, I was a young mother-to-be with a blue-collar husband headed up to the Slope. I hadn't yet envisioned running for elected office. But looking back, I can see that the tragedy planted a seed in me: If I ever had a chance to serve my fellow citizens, I would do so, and I'd work for the ordinary, hardworking people—like everyone who was a part of my ordinary, hardworking world."

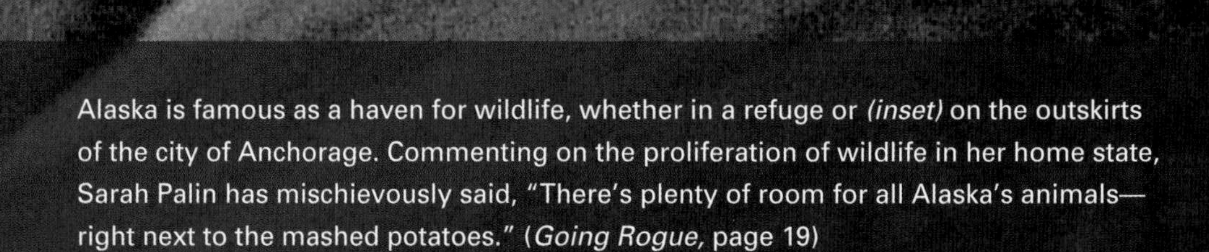

Alaska is famous as a haven for wildlife, whether in a refuge or *(inset)* on the outskirts of the city of Anchorage. Commenting on the proliferation of wildlife in her home state, Sarah Palin has mischievously said, "There's plenty of room for all Alaska's animals—right next to the mashed potatoes." (*Going Rogue,* page 19)

"Sarah Barracuda"

Growing up, Sarah spent her days going to school, playing the flute, and exploring Alaska's natural beauty, but her biggest love was sports. In high school she ran cross-country and played softball and basketball, paying for her equipment with money earned at various jobs in Wasilla. She also co-captained the local chapter of the Fellowship of Christian Athletes.

As a senior in high school, Sarah was the starting point guard and captain on Wasilla High's girls' basketball team. It was here that she earned the nickname "Sarah Barracuda" for her tenacity and competitive spirit. During the regional tournament, she injured her right ankle and was forced to leave the game. Still, the Wasilla Warriors prevailed and went on to the state championships. Sarah's injury affected her playing, but her hard work and leadership skills helped lead Wasilla to the championship.

Young Sarah Heath was an active participant in high school sports such as basketball, softball, and cross country. Here young Alaskan women of today's generation carry on the Wasilla sport tradition.

Enter Todd Palin

During her senior year, Sarah Heath met a boy who had just moved into Wasilla: a part–Yupik Eskimo named Todd Palin. Todd, who was working as a commercial fisherman while still a student, was instantly attracted to Sarah, and a courtship began.

After graduating high school, Sarah went to Hawaii Pacific University, and transferred to North Idaho College after one semester. In the summer of 1984, a family friend suggested that she enter the Miss Wasilla beauty pageant. At first she balked at the notion, but the temptation of winning money for college was tough to resist. Sarah easily won the competition, and moved on to the Miss Alaska pageant.

Sarah used the scholarship money to attend the University of Idaho, where she majored in journalism with an emphasis on broadcast news. The following summer, she finished third in the Miss Alaska competition, winning Miss Congeniality. She graduated with a bachelor's degree in communication in 1987 and moved to Anchorage, where she shared an apartment with her sister Heather.

During her time in college, Sarah continued her long-distance relationship with Todd, who was working as a fisherman in Alaska's Bristol Bay. They corresponded, talked on the telephone, and saw each other on vacations. On August 29, 1988, they walked into the Palmer Courthouse, where a magistrate pronounced them man and wife. They celebrated their first meal as a married couple at a Wendy's drive-through.

Todd moved in with Sarah and Heather, and the newlyweds began their life together. Sarah did customer service for the electric company while putting her communications degree to good use at a local television station part-time. Todd briefly worked as a baggage handler at Anchorage's airport before landing a job with BP Exploration Alaska on the North Slope. The job required him to be away from his new bride for seven days at a time as he worked in the oil fields.

(Preceding page) Jim Palin, Sarah's father-in-law, shares photographs of the beauty-queen competitor; a 1991 picture of her and husband Todd; and a prom photo from their dating days. *(Right)* Sarah Heath is all smiles after winning the 1984 Miss Wasilla beauty pageant.

Rising high above south central Alaska, Mount McKinley is the highest peak in North America. The mountain was named in 1897 by William Dickey in honor of the recent election of President William McKinley. It is also known to Alaskans as *Denali,* which means "The Great One" in Athabaskan, a language used by the native Koyukon tribe. The mountain is located in Denali National Park.

There are two peaks to Mount McKinley: a north and a south summit. The North Summit has an elevation of 19,470 feet, while the South Summit has an elevation of 20,320 feet. Five glaciers flow from the slopes.

Majestic Alaska: Mount McKinley

Mount McKinley was first successfully climbed when a party led by Hudson Stuck reached the summit on June 7, 1913. Walter Harper, Harry Karstens, and Robert Tatum comprised the rest of the group.

Mount McKinley is subject to some of the worst weather conditions in North America, having registered temperatures as low as -75 degrees as recently as 2003. Despite its harsh climate, the peak remains a popular destination for adventurous mountain climbers.

(Left) William McKinley, 25th president of the United States, was the last veteran of the American Civil War to be elected to the office. His tenure overlapped the 19th and 20th centuries and he presided over an era of prosperity—until he was assassinated in 1901. The popular president was later honored on a commemorative gold dollar (shown enlarged). He was also featured on the Series of 1934 $500 Federal Reserve Notes.

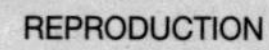

A view of Mount McKinley, or *Denali,* "The Great One." *(attached)* Hudson Stuck (1863–1920), an Episcopalian priest, was a co-leader of the first successful expedition up the South Peak of Mount McKinley. He and environmentalist John Muir share a feast day (April 22) on the calendar of saints of the Episcopal Church in the United States.

The Iditarod Trail Sled Dog Race is the most popular sporting event in Alaska, and is a symbol of the spirit and pride of Alaskans. The Iditarod features teams comprising up to 16 dogs and a "musher," racing a distance of 1,161 miles. The race, which begins on the first Saturday in March, usually takes approximately nine days to complete.

The Iditarod commences in downtown Anchorage with a ceremonial start, as teams head to Eagle River, 20 miles outside of the city. From there, the teams travel to Willow, where the race begins proper through the interior of Alaska, ending in Nome, on the west coast of the state.

In 1985, Libby Riddles, who later introduced Sarah Palin at her inauguration as governor, became the first woman to win the Iditarod. In 1992, Martin Buser of Switzerland became the first international winner of the race. Buser also currently holds the record for fastest time, completing the 2002 race in 8 days, 22 hours, 46 minutes, and 2 seconds.

The Iditarod was created in 1973 to commemorate the courageous run in 1925 to bring diphtheria serum to Nome when an outbreak threatened to wipe out the city. The relay used 20 mushers and 150 dogs, covering 674 miles in five and a half days despite subzero conditions.

Sporting Alaska: The Iditarod Trail Sled Dog Race

(Left) Three-time Iditarod champion Martin Buser of Big Lake, Alaska, drives his team out of the Ruby, Alaska, checkpoint and up the Yukon River (March 8, 2002). He would end up winning the race for a fourth time. *(Above)* Musher Libby Riddles stands in front of Nome's city hall, March 20, 1985. She crossed the finish line after driving her team through a blizzard to victory, becoming the first female champion of the Iditarod Trail Sled Dog Race.

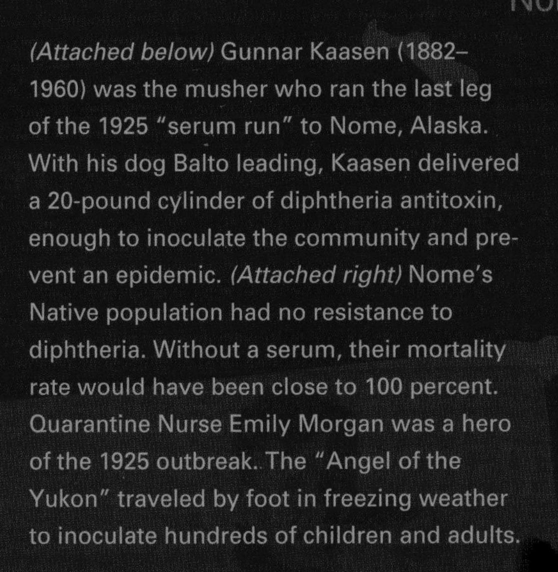

(Attached below) Gunnar Kaasen (1882–1960) was the musher who ran the last leg of the 1925 "serum run" to Nome, Alaska. With his dog Balto leading, Kaasen delivered a 20-pound cylinder of diphtheria antitoxin, enough to inoculate the community and prevent an epidemic. *(Attached right)* Nome's Native population had no resistance to diphtheria. Without a serum, their mortality rate would have been close to 100 percent. Quarantine Nurse Emily Morgan was a hero of the 1925 outbreak. The "Angel of the Yukon" traveled by foot in freezing weather to inoculate hundreds of children and adults.

The Palins added to their family when their son, Track, was born on April 20, 1989. Their second child, a daughter, Bristol, arrived on October 18, 1990. The names of their first two children reflect the Palins' love of sports. Track was born at the start of the spring track season. Bristol's name has two meanings, reflecting both Todd's work as a fisherman on his native Bristol Bay, and Sarah's young dream of working for the all-sports cable network ESPN, located in Bristol, Connecticut.

Beginning Public Service

In 1992, Sarah Palin was asked to run for a seat on the six-person Wasilla City Council. Although she was unfamiliar with the workings of local government, she wanted to have a say in the future direction of her hometown as it grew. She began a grassroots campaign, going door to door with Track and Bristol to state her case. Palin won the vote 530 to 310. Three years later she added her third child, Willow (born on July 5, 1994), to the mix, and she was elected to a second term on the city council by a vote of 413 to 185.

But Palin's second term on the city council didn't last long. In 1996, she decided to run for mayor against three-term incumbent John Stein. Palin campaigned on a platform of fresh ideas, free enterprise, lower property taxes, and fiscal responsibility. She also heavily promoted her social conservative values and activism in her church.

Although Wasilla elections are nonpartisan, the state Republican Party, in an unprecedented move in the city, ran advertisements on her behalf. Clearly they saw the 32-year-old dynamo as having a bright political future. On October 1, 1996, Sarah Palin was elected as the first female mayor of Wasilla, by a margin of 651 to 440.

Upon taking office, she set about reforming Wasilla's government. She made good on her campaign promises by cutting property taxes, improving the city's infrastructure, and taking a 10% pay cut. She held informal weekly meetings with residents at a local diner and randomly called citizens to find out how the government could better serve them.

(Left) Todd Palin and Sarah Heath married in August 1988. He is pictured laughing with fans at the Hays Days Grass Drags snowmachine event in Forest Lake, Minnesota, in 2008. Todd, a professional racer, is a four-time champion of Alaska's 1,971-mile Iron Dog snowmachine race. *(Opposite page)* Todd and Sarah in October 2006. In *Going Rogue,* she talks about them walking together at Wasilla High School's graduation ceremony. "Twenty-eight years later, we're still walking together, but maybe have picked up the pace a bit."

Sarah Palin

IN HER OWN Words

Feminism

"I'm a feminist who believes in equal rights and I believe that women certainly today have every opportunity that a man has to succeed and to try to do it all anyway. And I'm very, very thankful that I've been brought up in a family where gender hasn't been an issue."

—September 30, 2008, CBS News interview with Katie Couric

The Importance of Education

"Victor Hugo said, 'He who opens a school door, closes a prison.' It's a privileged obligation we have to open education doors. Every child, of every ability, is to be cherished and loved and taught. Every child provides this world hope."

—January 15, 2008, State of the State Address to the 25th Alaska Legislature

Ronald Reagan

"I'm thankful that I came of age politically in the era of Ronald Reagan, in high school and in college. He is my inspiration—his vision of America and of the exceptionalism of our country. I think about him every day. I think about what that Great Communicator has left our country and the rest of the world."

—September 17, 2008, Fox News interview on "Hannity & Colmes"

"I see the United States as being a force for good in the world—and, as Ronald Reagan used to talk about, America being the beacon of light and hope for those who are seeking democratic values and tolerance and freedom."

—September 24, 2008, CBS News interview with Katie Couric

Palin's first term was a rousing success, and in 1999 she cruised in her campaign for a second term as mayor, winning 73.6% of the vote. Later that year, she was elected president of the Alaska Conference of Mayors.

During her second term, Wasilla continued to grow according to Palin's vision for her hometown. Property taxes continued to be cut, and Wasilla received $8 million in federal funds for various projects, including a youth shelter and a railroad project.

By this time, the Palin family had expanded to six: Todd and Sarah's third daughter, Piper, was born on March 19, 2001.

Shortly before she left office in 2002, city residents approved the construction of Palin's crowning achievement as mayor. The $14.7 million Wasilla Multi-Use Sports Complex, a 102,000-square-foot complex containing an NHL-sized hockey rink, track, and artificial turf field, opened in 2004.

The center, which has a seating capacity of approximately 2,200 people, is home to the Alaska Avalanche of the North American Hockey League and the Arctic Predators of the American Indoor Football Association. In 2009, the entire facility was renamed in memory of Curtis D. Menard, a longtime Heath family friend and community leader. The center's hockey arena had already been named for Menard's son, Curtis Jr., who was killed in a plane crash in 2001.

Seeking Statewide Office

Term limits prevented Sarah Palin from seeking a third term as the mayor of Alaska's fastest-growing city. With her star rising as her time ran down, she thought it would be a good opportunity to test the waters of her appeal. She decided to run for the Republican nomination for lieutenant governor, but was unsuccessful, finishing second in the five-person primary. In her autobiography, *Going Rogue,* Palin would cite the demands of statewide campaigning while running Wasilla and raising a family, as well as her discomfort with fundraising, as the reasons for her loss.

The new governor, former longtime U.S. senator Frank Murkowski, appointed Palin to the Alaska Oil and Gas Conservation Commission as one of its three commissioners, as well as its chairman and ethics supervisor. It's possible that Murkowski thought he could give Palin, who campaigned heavily for him, a high-paying job so that he could add her to his long list of political cronies. But he soon found out that she could not be bought.

Shortly after taking office, she discovered that another commissioner, Randy Ruedrich, who was also Alaska's Republican Party chairman, was giving confidential information to a lobbyist of a corporation the AOGCC was supposed to be regulating. Even though it meant putting her political future on the line, Palin wrote to Murkowski, who eventually forced Ruedrich's resignation in November 2003. Palin did not stay on the commission much longer. Citing ethical lapses within the group, she resigned her position in January 2004.

(Left) Sarah Palin, mayor of Wasilla, Alaska, October 1996. *(Opposite page, left)* Sarah Palin's observations led to an ethics investigation into the activities of Randy Ruedrich of the Alaska Oil and Gas Conservation Commission. *(Opposite page, right)* The Palins' third daughter, Piper, was born in 2001. She is shown campaigning with her mother in 2006.

Palin
Ne
MOUNTAIN HARD WEAR
Palin Parnell

Born in Anchorage to a Mexican-American father and a Colombian mother, Scott Gomez is arguably the greatest hockey player ever to come from Alaska. Gomez, a center for the Montreal Canadiens, is the first native-born Alaskan, and the first Latino, to play in the National Hockey League.

Famous Alaskan:

Scott Gomez

Gomez was playing for the Tri-City Americans of the Western Hockey League when he was drafted by the New Jersey Devils in the first round of the 1998 NHL entry draft. In his first season with the Devils, he scored 19 goals and 51 assists, made the All-Star team, and was awarded the Calder Trophy as the league's best rookie. He scored 10 points in the playoffs as the Devils went on to win the Stanley Cup.

Over the next few years, Gomez would establish himself as one of the league's top playmakers. The Devils won the Stanley Cup again in 2002–2003, and he led the NHL in assists a year later, with 56.

A lockout forced the cancellation of the 2004–2005 season, but Gomez returned to Anchorage and signed with the Alaska Aces of the East Coast Hockey League. With 86 points in 61 games, he led the league in scoring and was named its Most Valuable Player.

When the NHL resumed in the fall of 2005, Gomez picked up where he had left off, scoring 33 goals and 84 points, both of which are career highs. After the 2006–2007

(Right) Gomez, #91 with the Montreal Canadiens, skates against the Carolina Hurricanes during the first period of an NHL hockey game in Raleigh, North Carolina, April 8, 2010.

season, Gomez moved across the Hudson River to sign with the New York Rangers, where he played two seasons before being traded to the Canadiens.

In international play, Gomez has played for the United States in four major tournaments. In 1998 and 1999, he played in the World Junior Championships. He won a bronze medal with the U.S. at the 2004 World Championships, and was a member of the 2006 Olympic hockey team.

In 2007, he was inducted as a charter member of the Alaska Sports Hall Of Fame.

(Left) Scott Gomez, suited up for the New York Rangers, prepares himself before a game against the Calgary Flames (January 2008). *(Below)* Governor Sarah Palin joins Cathy O'Connell (from Erdenheim, Pennsylvania), dropping the ceremonial puck between the New York Rangers' Scott Gomez, left, and the Philadelphia Flyers' Mike Richards, right, before the start of the October 11, 2008, NHL hockey game in Philadelphia.

Running for Governor

Palin spent the next year and a half concentrating on raising her family, being team manager to Track's hockey team, and figuring out her next political move. From 2003 to 2005, she served as one of three directors on Senator Ted Stevens's organization to recruit and train Republican women in Alaska for public service. She briefly considered running against Governor Murkowski's daughter, Lisa, for the Republican nomination for U.S. senator, but eventually decided against it.

Meanwhile, corruption continued in the state capital of Juneau, with the oil companies having undue influence over the government. Friends and strangers alike were contacting Palin, asking her to do something about it. On October 18, 2005, in her living room, Sarah Palin announced that she would seek the Republican nomination for governor of Alaska. The date was significant: not only was it Bristol's 15th birthday, but it was also Alaska Day, the state holiday commemorating the transfer of control of the Alaskan Territory from Russia to the United States in 1867.

Sarah holds her youngest daughter, Piper, 4, while talking with the media in her Wasilla home. It is Alaska Day—Tuesday, October 18, 2005—and Sarah has announced her candidacy for governor.

Sarah stands with Robert Robl and other supporters in the rain in Anchorage, Alaska, August 22, 2006. She is campaigning to win the Republican nomination to run for governor, facing former state legislator John Binkley of Fairbanks and incumbent Frank Murkowski. *(In pocket)* Palin gubernatorial campaign stickers.

(Above) Jewel sings her hit "You Were Meant for Me" at a USO holiday concert aboard the aircraft carrier USS *Harry S. Truman,* December 2000.

Famous Alaskan: Jewel Kilcher

Hailing from Homer, Alaska, Jewel Kilcher was one of the most successful musical acts of the 1990s. Best known by her first name, Jewel has sold 20 million records in the United States, with six Top Ten albums on the *Billboard* album chart.

As a child, Jewel often sang in bars with her Swiss-born father, who taught her how to yodel in the style of his countrymen, and she began writing songs at the age of 16. In the early 1990s, she moved to San Diego, where she lived in her van while honing her songwriting skills and performing in coffeehouses before being signed to Atlantic Records.

In 1995, Jewel released her debut record, *Pieces of You.* After a slow start, sales took off in 1996 and the album sold 12 million copies, spawning three hit singles: "Who Will Save Your Soul," "You Were Meant For Me," and "Foolish Games." *Pieces of You* was nominated for three Grammy awards and five MTV Video Music Awards (winning one). Jewel also won two *Billboard* awards, including #1 Female Singles Artist of 1997.

Her follow-up, 1998's *Spirit,* resulted in another Top Ten single, "Hands." Since then, Jewel has recorded several albums in different genres, including dance music, country, and children's music.

Jewel has written two books. In 1998, she released *A Night Without Armor,* a collection of her poems, which sold more than 1,000,000 copies and was a *New York Times* bestseller. Two years later, she published *Chasing Down the Dawn,* an autobiography filled with diary entries and stories about growing up in Alaska.

Jewel remains active as a recording artist, live performer, and television personality. She also devotes much of her time to charity work, including breast cancer awareness, education, and environmental causes. She married world champion rodeo cowboy Ty Murray in 1998.

(Left) Jewel's husband, Ty Murray, is considered by many fans to be the greatest rodeo champion in history.

Jewel performs with her father, Atz Kilcher, during her August 20, 2009, concert in Anchorage, Alaska.

Famous Alaskan: Ted Stevens

One of the most influential American politicians of the last half century, Ted Stevens served Alaska in the U.S. Senate from 1968 to 2008, and is the most important legislator in the state's history. Only six other men in American history have served in the Senate longer than Stevens.

Born in 1923 in Indianapolis, Indiana, Stevens joined the Army in 1943, during World War II. Trained as a pilot, he flew transport planes behind enemy lines in the China Burma India theater, against the Japanese. He was awarded the Distinguished Flying Cross, the Air Medal, and the Yuan Hai Medal, which was given by the Chinese government.

Upon discharge, Stevens attended college at UCLA and Harvard Law School. In 1953, after working in Washington, D.C., he accepted a position with an Alaskan law firm and moved to Fairbanks. Shortly thereafter, he was named the U.S. attorney for the territory.

In 1956, Stevens returned to Washington to work for the Department of the Interior. He took up the cause of Alaskan statehood; Alaska, as a territory, was under the jurisdiction of his department. He worked closely with President Dwight D. Eisenhower to address national-security concerns because of its proximity to Soviet Russia. Stevens helped write the Alaska Statehood Act, which was signed into law by Eisenhower on July 7, 1958. Alaska officially entered the Union as the 49th state on January 3, 1959.

After serving two terms in the Alaska House of Representatives, Stevens was appointed to the U.S. Senate in 1968, following the death of Bob Bartlett. From 1977 to 1985 he served as the Republican whip, a position that requires leadership and respect. During his 40-year career in the Senate, Stevens chaired many committees, including Appropriations, Governmental Affairs, and Ethics. He lost his bid for an eighth term in 2008.

In 2000, Ted Stevens was voted Alaskan of the Century, and the Anchorage International Airport was renamed in his honor.

Tragically, he died in an airplane accident in August 2010.

(Right) Senator Stevens and his wife, Catherine Ann Chandler, get to know a panda bear during a 2007 visit to the National Zoo in Washington, DC.

STEVENS, Theodore F. (Ted). (1923–2010)

from the Biographical Directory of the United States Congress

Senate Years of Service: 1968–2009
Party: Republican

STEVENS, Theodore F. (Ted), a senator from Alaska; born in Indianapolis, Marion County, Indiana, November 18, 1923 • Attended Oregon State College and Montana State College; graduated, University of California, Los Angeles, 1947; graduated, Harvard Law School, 1950 • Served in the United States Army Air Corps in the Second World War, in China, 1943–1946 • Admitted to the bar in California in 1950, to the District of Columbia bar in 1951, and to the Alaska bar in 1957 • Practiced law in Fairbanks, Alaska, 1953 • Legislative counsel, Department of Interior, Washington, DC, 1956 • Assistant to the secretary of the interior, 1958 • Chief counsel, Department of the Interior, 1960 • Returned to Anchorage, Alaska, in 1961 and practiced law • Elected to state house of representatives in 1964; reelected in 1966, serving as speaker pro tempore and majority leader • Appointed on December 24, 1968, as a Republican to the United States Senate to fill the vacancy caused by the death of E.L. Bartlett, and was subsequently elected in a special election on November 3, 1970, to complete the unexpired term ending January 3, 1973 • Reelected in 1972, 1978, 1984, 1990, 1996, and 2002 (served from December 24, 1968, to January 3, 2009) • Republican whip (1977–1985); president pro tempore (2003–2007); chair, Republican Senatorial Campaign Committee (94th Congress), Select Committee on Ethics (98th and 99th Congresses), Committee on Rules and Administration (104th Congress [January 3, 1995–September 12, 1995]), Committee on Governmental Affairs (104th Congress [September 12, 1995–January 2, 1997]), Committee on Appropriations (105th and 106th Congresses, 1[illegible]th Congress [January 20, 2001–June 6, 2001], 108th Congress); Committee on Commerce, Science and Transportation (109th Congress).

(Below) Stevens escorts former first lady Nancy Reagan, along with Lt. General Frank G. Klotz, at the dedication ceremony of the Ronald W. Reagan Missile Defense Site, April 10, 2006.

Anchorage, Alaska, October 23, 2006: Sarah Palin reviews her notes before a gubernatorial debate. In the foreground, former governor Tony Knowles (seeking a third term) chats with Independent candidate Andrew Halco ("a wealthy, effete young chap who had taken over his father's local Avis Rent A Car, and . . . starred in his own car commercials," as Palin describes him in *Going Rogue*).

(Photo) Palin shakes hands with former Alaska governor Tony Knowles after a debate in Anchorage, Alaska, Monday, October 23, 2006. (Green Party of Alaska gubernatorial candidate David Massie is in front.) *(Attached)* Palin's conservative "red meat" principles helped propel her to the Alaska governor's mansion. Later they would resonate with a national audience.

OPTICS• U.S.A. C91898

The nomination would not be easy to achieve. Governor Murkowski's approval rating was down, but he still had considerable advantages in name recognition, fundraising capabilities, and the backing of the Alaskan GOP machine. There was also a challenge from former state senator John Binkley.

Palin used her outsider status to her advantage, promising ethics reform, conservative principles, and increased private-sector development of energy resources. She also picked up a key endorsement from popular former governor Walter Hickel. The strategy worked, as Palin won the nomination with 50.6% of the vote. Murkowski finished a distant third, with only 19.1%.

In the gubernatorial election, Palin made clear the differences between herself and her challengers, Democratic former governor Tony Knowles and Andrew Halcro, a former Republican state representative running as an Independent. Her themes, "New Energy For Alaska" and "Take A Stand," reflected the need for a change in government, led by someone with a history of reform, with no ties to Big Oil.

On November 7, 2006, Sarah Palin was elected governor of Alaska—the first woman to hold the position and, at 42, its youngest-ever chief executive. She won 48% of the vote, while Knowles carried 41%, with Halcro a distant third at 9.5%.

(Preceding page) Sarah holds her daughter, Piper, as they watch the gubernatorial polling results in Anchorage, Alaska. The date is November 7, 2006. Sarah Palin will soon be the Frontier State's next governor. *(Right)* Mayor, and now governor, Sarah Palin.

Chapter 2

Governor Sarah Palin

Governor Sarah Palin talks about the process she went through to choose Alaska's state quarter design. The coin was unveiled in Anchorage on April 23, 2007, and the U.S. Mint released it into

(Above) In Fairbanks, Superior Court Judge Niesje Steinkruger swears in Sarah Palin as governor of Alaska. Todd holds the Bible during the December 4, 2006, inauguration ceremony.

Two months after the election, Sarah Palin was sworn in as governor. In a nod to the city where the state constitution was written, the inauguration took place in Fairbanks instead of the state capital of Juneau. Also symbolic was her introduction by Libby Riddles, the first woman to win the famous Iditarod sled dog race, which, for much of its history, began in Palin's hometown of Wasilla.

Palin began her inaugural address by praising Riddles for being "an underdog, a risk taker . . . an outsider . . . bold and tough," and adding, "She shattered an ice ceiling." Then Palin repeated the issues central to her victory: a common-sense energy plan, less government intervention, fiscal responsibility, and a brighter future for Alaska's children.

(Above) Palin signs her oath-of-office document in the presence of Lieutenant Governor Sean Parnell and Superior Court Judge Niesje Steinkruger. *(Right)* Sarah, Todd, Bristol, 16, and Piper, 5, stand as the colors are retired at the end of an inauguration ceremony in Fairbanks, Alaska, December 4, 2006. "Piper was as patient as most five-year-olds could be," Sarah writes in *Going Rogue,* "but could barely muster one last hand on the heart at the end of the ceremony."

SarahPalin

Abortion

"I'll do all I can to see every baby is created with a future and potential. The legislature should do all it can to protect human life."

—*August 29, 2008, question-and-answer with Mike Coppock, Newsmax.com*

"I am pro-life. With the exception of a doctor's determination that the mother's life would end if the pregnancy continued. I believe that no matter what mistakes we make as a society, we cannot condone ending another life."

—*July 31, 2006, Eagle Forum Gubernatorial Candidate Questionnaire*

Small Business

"Alaska's small-business owners are the backbone of our regional economies. Small Alaskan-owned businesses should have just as much say in state policy as the big companies do. Our precious businesses are major employers of Alaskans and keep Alaska's money circulating through our economy. As mayor and CEO of the booming city of Wasilla, my team invited investment and encouraged business growth by eliminating small-business inventory taxes, eliminated personal property taxes, reduced real property tax mill levies every year I was in office, reduced fees, and built the infrastructure our businesses needed to grow and prosper."

—*November 3, 2006, Palin–Parnell campaign booklet, New Energy for Alaska*

THE SEAL OF THE STATE
OF ALASKA

An End to "Politics As Usual"

The new governor's first order of business was to make good on her promise to clean up the state capital. In the summer of 2006, federal agents raided the offices of six members of the Alaska legislature as part of a corruption probe that had begun two years earlier. The investigation dealt with lawmakers who were receiving illegal campaign contributions from the VECO Corporation, an oil field-services company. The culture of corruption in Juneau was so deep and so out in the open that the legislators even had hats proclaiming themselves to be members of the "CBC," or "Corrupt Bastards Club."

It didn't matter to her that most of the members of the CBC were fellow Republicans. As she had proved during her time with the AOGCC, Palin was committed to ridding Alaska's government of those who had abused the public trust and were in the pockets of the special-interest corporations.

On the third day of the legislative session, Palin sent her proposal to drastically overhaul Alaska's ethics and disclosure laws. Although she faced opposition from her own party, she reached across the aisle to Democratic lawmakers. In July 2007, she signed into law a bill that restricted lobbyists, improved disclosure laws, and changed the ethics laws in both the legislative and executive branches.

Palin further separated her administration from that of her predecessor that summer, when she sold a jet that Governor Murkowski had purchased with state funds in 2005. The 10-seat Westwind II, which cost $2.7 million and an additional $50,000 a month in maintenance, was seen as a symbol of the free-spending, corrupt days that preceded her arrival in Juneau.

Her original plan was to sell the plane on the online auction site eBay.com, but after three attempts, she was unable to find a buyer willing to pay the minimum bid. Eventually, she put the transaction in the hands of a broker, who sold it to a businessman from Valdez for $2.1 million. It was yet another example of the bold ideas that Sarah Palin was bringing to her attempts to shape Alaska's future.

(Opposite page) Sarah Palin shakes hands as she walks with Piper, 5 (foreground center), Todd, and Willow, 12 (background center), after an inauguration ceremony in Fairbanks, Alaska, December 4, 2006. *(Right)* Sarah and Todd dance at the inaugural ball in Juneau, Alaska, January 20, 2007. Nearly 800 people showed up to greet the governor and her family at the first of six inaugural balls planned throughout Alaska.

When Sarah Palin was running for her second term as mayor of Wasilla, her opponent called her a "cheerleader" during a debate. Palin took offense at the comment, because she wasn't a cheerleader; she was a jock.

Sarah originally went to college to pursue a career as a sportscaster, with the goal of working for ESPN. She graduated from the University of Idaho with a degree in broadcast journalism and briefly worked as a sportscaster in Anchorage after graduation. She named her second child Bristol after the Connecticut town where ESPN has its headquarters.

(Below) February 11, 2007, Big Lake, Alaska: Sarah Palin drops the starting flag for the first team out—Todd and Kyle Malamute of Fairbanks—in the 2,000-mile Iron Dog snowmobile race. Twenty-eight teams left the starting line for the 1,100-mile ride to Nome before heading to the finish in Fairbanks.

Sports have always played a huge role in Sarah Palin's life. In the mid-1970s, Chuck and Sally Heath took up running, and they passed down their love of the sport to their children. Chuck also coached track at Wasilla High and often took neighborhood kids to Anchorage for track meets.

Palin has remained an avid runner, preferring to run up to 10 miles a day. Her oldest son was named Track because he was born at the start of the spring track season. In 2005, at the age of 41 and after having given birth to four children, Palin ran the Humpy's Marathon in Anchorage. She completed with a time of 3:59:36, which was fourth in her age group and 63rd place overall.

When Sarah was a child, her father often took her on hunting trips before school. She is a longtime member of the National Rifle Association and a strong proponent of Second Amendment rights.

Sarah Palin and Sports

The two team sports with which Sarah Palin is most closely associated are basketball and hockey. As a senior in high school, she was the starting point guard for the Wasilla Warriors, earning the nickname "Sarah Barracuda" for her toughness and determination. Her team went on to win the state championship, despite Sarah's playing on an injured ankle. She was also the captain of the local chapter of the Fellowship of Christian Athletes.

As for hockey, Palin is not known to play the sport, but she is a self-described "hockey mom." In 2004 she chose not to run for the U.S. Senate so that she could stay at home and be the manager of Track's team. During the campaign, she dropped the ceremonial first puck at the Philadelphia Flyers' season opener against the New York Rangers.

(Above) Sarah tries on a pair of running shoes from Sarah Emberley at Joe King's shoe store in Concord, New Hampshire, October 15, 2008.

Governor Palin greets Philadelphia Flyers captain Mike Richards before a ceremonial puck drop before the start of an NHL hockey game with the New York Rangers, October 11, 2008.

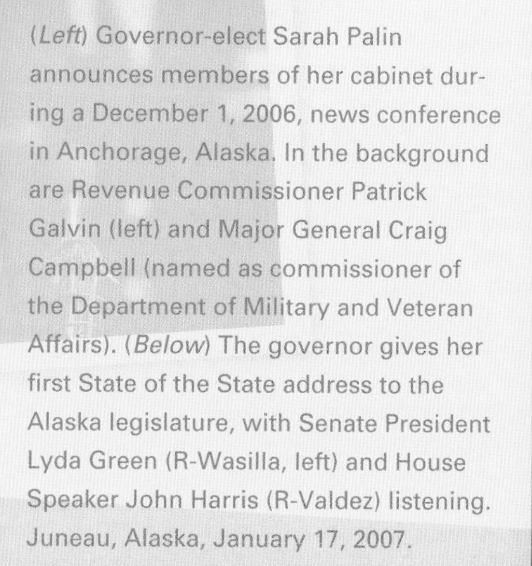

(*Left*) Governor-elect Sarah Palin announces members of her cabinet during a December 1, 2006, news conference in Anchorage, Alaska. In the background are Revenue Commissioner Patrick Galvin (left) and Major General Craig Campbell (named as commissioner of the Department of Military and Veteran Affairs). (*Below*) The governor gives her first State of the State address to the Alaska legislature, with Senate President Lyda Green (R-Wasilla, left) and House Speaker John Harris (R-Valdez) listening. Juneau, Alaska, January 17, 2007.

(*Above*) The governor-elect talks on the phone at her transition office in Anchorage, Alaska, December 1, 2006. At the age of 42, she would soon be sworn in as Alaska's youngest (and first woman) governor.

The State of Alaska's jet is seen here by the Alaska Army National Guard hanger in Juneau, shortly after arriving Tuesday night, November 8, 2005. The 1984 Westwind II was put to immediate use by Governor Frank Murkowski for state business. The Alaska State Department of Public Safety purchased the jet for more than $2 million. Governor Palin saw it as an unnecessary expense—so she sold it.

Lieutenant Colonel David Osborn (center) and Command Sergeant Major Alan Feaster (right) of the Alaska Army National Guard unit 3-297 infantry battalion present Governor Palin with a flag the unit flew from an Army gun truck while deployed in Iraq. The presentation, in honor of her support of the military, takes place at Fort Richardson, in Anchorage, Alaska, November 19, 2007.

Todd Palin carries Trig at the governor's picnic, July 25, 2009, in Anchorage. "I hadn't known what to expect," Sarah would later write in *Going Rogue*. "I didn't know what [Trig] would look like or how I would feel. But when I saw him, my heart was flooded with unspeakable joy. I knew that not only had God made Trig different but He had made him perfect."

Down Syndrome

Sarah Palin's youngest son, Trig, was born with Down syndrome, a genetic condition that affects approximately 6,000 births every year. It occurs more frequently when the baby's mother is over 40 years old, when it affects about 1 in 100 births. Down syndrome can be diagnosed during pregnancy through an amniocentesis. The condition is named for John Langdon Down, the English physician who first diagnosed it in 1862.

People with Down syndrome develop physically and mentally slower than those without the condition, with IQs generally in the 35 to 70 range. Their cognitive development, including speech and motor skills, is impaired. They share distinctive physical characteristics, including a small chin, almond-shaped eyes, and low muscle tone.

The condition is caused by abnormalities with Chromosome 21, and there are three variations of the disorder: Trisomy 21, the most common variation; Mosaic Down syndrome; and Translocation Down syndrome. Trig Palin was born with Trisomy 21.

There is no cure or prevention for Down syndrome. Individuals with the disability have a greater risk of congenital heart disease, Celiac disease, and leukemia. However, with early intervention, including speech and physical therapy, Down syndrome children can lead productive lives well into adulthood. Depending on the severity of the condition, they can be expected to live into their 50s.

(Left) Teresa Gattuso hugs Sarah as Annie Callahan, right, looks on during an election rally at Deep Run High school in Richmond, Virginia, November 1, 2008. Both children have Down syndrome.

Taking On Big Oil

Another main priority was to approve the construction of a pipeline to stretch from the natural-gas reserves at Prudhoe Bay on the North Slope to Calgary, Alberta, Canada, a distance of 1,715 miles. In Calgary, the gasline would connect with existing lines that transported the fuel to the United States. The gasline was originally authorized in the late 1970s, but its construction had been placed on hold for various reasons over the years.

(Above) Governor Palin is flanked by Steve Smith (left), a 69-year-old fisherman from Cordova, Alaska, and Mike Webber, a 47-year-old Native Alaskan artist and fisherman. They're at the National Press Club in Washington, DC, February 28, 2006, at a news conference held by the "Whole Truth" campaign in support of victims of the *Exxon Valdez* oil spill. The following day, a class-action lawsuit, *Exxon v. Baker*, will be argued in the U.S. Supreme Court.

Rather than give the job to the Big Oil firms with whom she had clashed while on the AOGCC, Palin endorsed the Alaska Gasline Inducement Act, signed in July 2007, which opened the bidding up to other firms. The AGIA overwhelmingly passed the Alaska legislature, and the license was awarded, a year later, to a company outside the Big Oil corporations. (The gasline is expected to open in 2018, with a projected cost of $26 billion.) In only a few months in office, Palin had accomplished what no Alaskan governor had been able to do in 30 years, and her approval rating was 93%.

Palin further took on Big Oil in December 2007, when she imposed a 2.5% windfall tax on the net profit of every barrel produced in Alaska. The tax added an estimated $6 billion to the state's coffers. Six months later, she redistributed $741 million of the tax revenue to Alaska's citizens to help them cope with the rising cost of energy as winter loomed.

Visiting the Troops

In July 2007, Sarah Palin left North America for the first time when she visited with U.S. military personnel stationed in Kuwait. As part of the two-day tour, she posed for pictures with members of the Alaska National Guard, took shots at a firing range, and learned more about the war effort. On the return trip to Alaska, she stopped in Germany, visiting the Ramstein Air Base for breakfast, following it with a trip to Landstuhl Regional Medical Center in Germany to meet with wounded troops.

Six weeks after her trip overseas, Palin's oldest son, Track, who had recently turned 18, enlisted in the U.S. Army. He was sworn in as an infantryman on September 11, 2007. (Shortly after his mother was chosen to be John McCain's presidential running mate, Track's unit would be deployed to Iraq for 12 months of service.)

March 2007, Juneau, Alaska: Governor Palin stands with state commissioners and industry representatives as she introduces the Alaska Gasline Inducement Act.

Governor Palin shakes hands with members of Company B, 3rd Battalion, 297th Infantry Regiment, Alaska National Guard, during her July 2007 visit to Camp Virginia, Kuwait. She concluded her two-day trip with a tour and lunch at the camp and a tour of the Life Support Area-Kuwait Rapid Fielding Initiative facility.

In order to deal in private with the challenges now facing her family, Sarah did not publicly disclose her pregnancy until her seventh month.

One month later, Sarah and Todd Palin were in Dallas for an oil-and-gas conference when she went into labor, even though the baby wasn't expected for another five weeks. After consulting with her doctor back home, Sarah determined she was well enough to give her speech before flying back to Wasilla. On April 18, 2008, Trig Palin was born.

Just three days later, Sarah Palin had returned to her Anchorage office, tackling the problems facing Alaska. But in a few months, her life would be permanently turned inside out.

Enter John McCain

In February 2008, Sarah Palin attended a National Governors Association conference in Washington, D.C. At a reception, she and Todd met Arizona senator John McCain and his wife, Cindy. They spoke briefly, bonding over the fact that both couples had sons in the military. To the casual observer, it appeared to be nothing more than mere cocktail-party chatter.

But few such meetings in Washington, D.C., happen by chance. McCain had already taken a commanding lead in the race for the Republican nomination for president, which he would clinch a few weeks later. His search for a running mate had already begun, and he was impressed by Palin's record of reform and willingness to fight for her beliefs, even if it meant upsetting fellow Republicans.

As the summer passed, speculation grew about who would share the ticket with McCain. Among the names tossed about were those of Governor Tim Pawlenty of Minnesota and Senator Lindsey Graham of South Carolina. It was even suspected that McCain would ask his good friend Senator Joe Lieberman (who had been a Democrat until 2006, when he was reelected as an Independent).

On August 25, 2008, John McCain personally called Sarah Palin, who was at the Alaska State Fair, and asked her to fly down to Arizona for an interview. Three days later, she was at the Flagstaff home of a close friend of McCain's, where she met with two top members of McCain's staff. Over the course of the day, she was grilled about everything from foreign policy to her religious beliefs to her public and private life.

The next morning, Palin traveled to McCain's home in Sedona, Arizona, where she met with the Vietnam War hero on the deck of his house. After chatting with her, he walked over to his advisors to confer with them, then returned to Palin and asked her to be his running mate.

(Left) April 23, 2008: Sarah and Todd hold their baby boy, Trig, just five days old. *(Opposite page)* Palin and McCain met at a February 2008 National Governors Association conference in Washington, DC. She was vice chair of the association's Natural Resources Committee.

Intriguing Conservative:

John McCain

The man who brought Sarah Palin into the national spotlight, Arizona senator John McCain, has given a lifetime of service to the United States of America. One of the most unusual individuals in Republican politics, his career has been long distinguished by his desire to put, as his 2008 presidential campaign slogan said, "Country First."

John Sidney McCain III was born on August 29, 1936, in the Panama Canal Zone. At the time, his father was serving in the U.S. Navy, eventually rising, like his father before him, to the rank of four-star admiral. As with many members of military families, McCain moved around the world depending on where his father was stationed.

After his graduation from high school, McCain, following the career paths of his father and grandfather, enrolled in the U.S. Naval Academy in Annapolis, Maryland. As a cadet he frequently clashed with his superiors, and he took up boxing. His willingness to speak his mind and to stand up for himself would later define McCain's public life as a self-proclaimed "maverick."

Trained as a fighter pilot, he shipped off to Vietnam as a lieutenant commander in 1967. On his 23rd bombing mission, his plane was shot down and he was captured by the North Vietnamese. McCain was repeatedly tortured by his captors. When he was offered an early release because of his father's status as commander of U.S. forces in Vietnam, he refused to leave unless all of his fellow prisoners were released. In March 1973, after five and a half years in the infamous "Hanoi Hilton" prison, John McCain was released.

(Right) The U.S. Navy training base known as McCain Field was commissioned and named in honor of Admiral John S. McCain, July 14, 1961, in Meridian, Mississippi. Here, Lieutenant John S. McCain III stands in front of his grandfather's portrait with his parents, Rear Admiral John S. McCain Jr. and Roberta Wright McCain.

(Right) September 14, 1973: John McCain is greeted by President Richard Nixo[illegible] Washington, after spen[illegible] more than five years in [illegible] Vietnamese prisoner-[illegible] camp known as the "Hanoi Hilton." McCain had been released in March 1973.

The year is 2008. More than three decades have passed since he returned from Vietnam, and John McCain has built a reputation of service to the nation. He is a U.S. senator and the Republican Party's presidential candidate. Here he speaks at the NAACP Annual Convention held at the Duke Energy Center in Cincinnati, Wednesday, July 16, 2008.

McCain returned to the United States, where he underwent physical therapy for his injuries and served on a base in Florida and as the Navy's liaison to the Senate. He retired from the Navy as a captain in 1981, having earned 17 awards and decorations for his heroism.

In 1982, the retired Navy officer was elected to the U.S. House of Representatives from Arizona's first district. After serving two terms, he was elected to the U.S. Senate, replacing conservative legend Barry Goldwater, who was retiring.

Throughout his career in the Senate, John McCain has been a vocal critic of the influence of special-interest groups in government, speaking out against pork barrel spending, and supporting campaign-finance reform. His experience in the military has also made him one of the most respected senators on foreign policy. In times when the Republicans have held a majority in the Senate, he has chaired the Senate Commerce and Indian Affairs Committees.

John McCain first ran for president in 2000. Traveling the country on a bus dubbed the Straight Talk Express, he took his message directly to the people. He won several early primaries, but eventually lost out to George W. Bush, who went on to become the 43rd president of the United States.

Following his defeat, McCain returned to the Senate, where his habit of speaking his mind and his bipartisanship led him to have very high approval ratings nationwide. He was easily reelected to a fourth Senate term in 2004, before his unsuccessful 2008 presidential campaign.

John McCain is married to the former Cindy Hensley. They have a daughter, Meghan, who is a Republican columnist and commentator, and two sons, John McCain IV and Jimmy, who have chosen to follow their forefathers into the military. In 1993 the McCains adopted a daughter, Bridget, from an orphanage run by Mother Teresa. John McCain also has three children from his first marriage.

Senator McCain has written five books, all of which draw upon his own story or those of people who have lived honorable, courageous, and extraordinary lives.

(Above) Senator McCain and his wife Cindy arrive for his post-primary election victory party in Nashua, New Hampshire, January 8, 2008.

Chapter 3

The Race for the White House

Vice-presidential candidate Sarah Palin acknowledges the crowd as she prepares to address the Republican National Convention in St. Paul, Minnesota, Wednesday, September 3, 2008.

JOHN COLE
©THE TIMES-TRIBUNE
SCRANTON PA
CAGLECARTOONS.
COM
NOW MUSH!
CRACK
LISSEN TO TH' LADY, MY FRIENDS.
PALIN
REFORM

JOHNCOLE
©THE TIMES-TRIBUNE
SCRANTON PA
CAGLECARTOONS.
COM
NOW MUSH!
CRACK
LISSEN TO TH' LADY, MY FRIENDS.
PALIN
REFORM

The Republican candidates shake hands during the "Road to the Convention Rally" at the Erwin J. Nutter Center in Dayton, Ohio, August 29, 2008.

Palin greets admirers after leaving the stage of the Dayton rally.

On August 29, 2008, Sarah Palin was introduced to the country at a John McCain rally in Dayton, Ohio. It was not only McCain's 72nd birthday, but also Sarah and Todd Palin's 20th wedding anniversary. August 29 was also the day after the Democratic National Convention, where Senator Barack Obama had accepted the nomination in front of 84,000 people in Denver.

The Palin announcement stole the thunder from Obama's speech, dominating the news cycle throughout the weekend. Little was known about the young woman standing with McCain or about her family, and the press went to work in trying to dig up as much information as possible. Everything from Palin's political positions to her personal life was discussed in the media, as both allies and enemies were dispatched to put their desired spin on the new vice-presidential nominee.

(Above) Four-month-old Trig Palin seems amazed by the scene, held by his mother after she addressed the Republican National Convention in St. Paul, Minnesota, September 3, 2008. *(Left)* Track Palin watches the proceedings of the convention.

Governor Palin and Cindy McCain applaud during a campaign rally in Hershey, Pennsylvania, October 28, 2008.

Intriguing Conservative: Cindy McCain

A politician's wife is often seen by her husband's side, rarely saying anything. But Cindy McCain, the wife of Senator John McCain, is an accomplished businesswoman and philanthropist in her own right.

Cindy Hensley was born in 1954 in Phoenix, Arizona. Her father founded Hensley & Co. and turned it into one of the largest beer distributors in the United States. Cindy didn't enter the family business early, choosing instead to pursue a career in special education, earning a master's degree from the University of Southern California in 1978.

At a military reception in Hawaii in 1979, Cindy met John McCain, then the U.S. Navy liaison to the Senate. The couple married in May 1980. Four years later, their first child, Meghan, was born, followed by John Sidney "Jack" McCain IV in 1986 and James McCain in 1988.

Mrs. McCain founded the American Voluntary Medical Team in 1988 to organize medical trips to Third World countries that had been ravaged by war or natural disaster. Three years later, she was working with Mother Teresa's orphanage in Bangladesh when she met two infants who needed stronger medical attention than was readily available. She brought them to America. The McCain family adopted one of the girls, whom they named Bridget, and arranged for a family friend to adopt the other.

After the AVMT ceased operations in 1995, McCain split her time between raising her family, doing charity work, and helping to run Hensley & Co., of which she became the chair in 2000. She owns, with her children, a stake in the Arizona Diamondbacks baseball team. On the final night of the 2008 Republican National Convention, she introduced the seven McCain children and spoke of her husband's love of America.

Cindy McCain, wife of Republican presidential candidate John McCain, poses on stage with the McCain children before speaking at the Republican National Convention in St. Paul, Minnesota, September 4, 2008. From left: Meghan, Andy, Jimmy, Cindy, Jack, Doug, Bridget, and Sidney.

As a result, there was one aspect of her family life that the Palins could no longer keep private. On the morning of the first day of the Republican National Convention, the Palins were forced to disclose that their 17-year-old daughter, Bristol, had gotten pregnant outside of marriage. Her son, Tripp Johnston, would be born on December 27, 2008.

Talk of the Town

From Ohio, it was on to the Xcel Energy Center in St. Paul, Minnesota, for the convention. On the evening of September 3, Senate Minority Leader Mitch McConnell of Kentucky conducted the formal adoption and announcement of the vice-presidential nominee. After nearly a week of rumors, distortions, and half-truths, it was time for the country to hear Sarah Palin in her own words.

Her speech touched all the bases to resonate with conservative America. Palin began by thanking and praising John McCain for his courage and devotion to his country. Then, she moved on to talk about her family life, including Track's and her nephew's military service and how much joy she gets from being the mother of a special-needs child.

Seeing a handful of delegates wearing hockey jerseys in the crowd, Palin went off her script. She gave a shout-out to hockey moms and then brought down the house by saying, "You know, they say the difference between a hockey mom and a pit bull? Lipstick."

When the laughter died down, she told her story of going from the Wasilla PTA to the state house in Juneau. She told of her record of ethics reform, fiscal restraint, and going against the establishment and the special-interest groups.

She then cited her experience on the North Slope when stating that reducing America's dependence on foreign oil is crucial to national security, and that it could only happen by increasing off-shore drilling. The audience, taking up Rudy Giuliani's mantra from earlier in the evening, began chanting, "Drill, baby, drill!"

Along the way, Palin took plenty of shots at the Democrats and Barack Obama—his inexperience as an executive, and his plan for the country. With every blow she landed, the crowd roared its approval. Palin had them in the palm of her hand.

(Left) Chuck and Sally Heath are acknowledged by their daughter—and by the audience of enthusiastic delegates—at the convention.

Republican delegates show their support as Sarah Palin addresses the national convention in St. Paul.

LEAVE ME ALONE

Wasilla, September 3, 2008: Alaskans Scott Myers and Judith Gregory emotionally wipe their eyes after watching Sarah Palin accept the Republican nomination for vice president. *(In envelope)* A transcript of Sarah Palin's Republican National Convention nomination acceptance speech.

Governor Palin is escorted by Colonel Daly during a deployment ceremony for the 1st Stryker Brigade Combat Team, 25th Infantry Division, at Fort Wainwright in Fairbanks, Alaska. The date is September 11, 2008, and Palin's son Track is being deployed with the team to Iraq.

She closed with a moving story of John McCain's courage and leadership seen through the eyes of Tom Moe, who was in the crowd. Moe was a prisoner of war in the "Hanoi Hilton" prison camp in North Vietnam, with John McCain. Every day, after being tortured, McCain would smile and give a thumbs-up as he passed Moe on the way back to his cell. The gesture reminded Moe that, despite their current situation, eventually they would pull through.

The crowd was touched as Palin finished the speech. Cheers rang out in the arena, and she was joined onstage by Todd, four of her children (Track was preparing to deploy to Iraq), and, in a surprise appearance, John McCain and his family. Forty minutes after taking the stage, Sarah Palin was now the talk of the town.

The next day at the convention, McCain formally accepted the Republican Party nomination, and the general election was officially underway.

(Below) Sarah Palin, holding her son Trig, is joined by the rest of the family onstage after her Republican National Convention speech. From left: her son Track; daughter Bristol and Bristol's boyfriend, Levi Johnston; daughters Willow and Piper; and husband, Todd.

When tensions grew high during Sarah Palin's preparation for her debate with Joe Biden, she received help from an unlikely source: Senator Joe Lieberman of Connecticut. Lieberman, an old friend of his Senate colleague John McCain, offered words of support and encouragement to the Alaska governor.

Lieberman made history in 2000 when, as Al Gore's running mate, he became the first Jewish candidate on a major political-party ticket. Gore lost the election to George W. Bush in one of the tightest and most controversial races in American history.

Lieberman was first elected to the Senate in 1988, after serving six years as Connecticut's attorney general. Throughout his career he's developed a reputation for reaching across the political aisle, particularly on foreign-policy issues.

In 2006, his unwavering support for the war in Iraq caused Lieberman to lose the Democratic primary in his bid for reelection. He chose to reenter the race as an Independent, and he won by getting a large percentage of the Republican and Independent vote. However, he is part of the Senate Democratic Caucus, and he chairs the Committee on Homeland Security and Governmental Affairs.

During the 2008 presidential campaign, Lieberman further angered Democrats by endorsing John McCain, who strongly considered him for the vice-presidential nomination. Lieberman spoke at the Republican National Convention.

(Above) Senator Joe Lieberman speaks to supporters at VFW Post 5095 in East Hampton, Connecticut, September 25, 2006. Lieberman argued that setting a timeline for the United States to leave Iraq would leave our nation more vulnerable to terrorism.

Intriguing Independent: Joe Lieberman

John McCain is greeted by Joe Lieberman at a town-hall meeting at Exeter Town Hall in Exeter, New Hampshire, March 12, 2008.

On the Campaign Trail

Sarah Palin's performance at the Republican National Convention resonated throughout the country. The conservative base, which had not yet warmed up to McCain because of comments he had made in the past, was energized. The size of the crowds at rallies grew exponentially, campaign contributions skyrocketed, and McCain took the lead in the polls, all because of the charismatic Alaskan. After having been in government for 15 years, Sarah Palin was suddenly an overnight sensation.

Following her performance at the convention, she was sent out on the campaign trail, where she came face to face with thousands of Americans who were captivated by her message. But after a week on the road, she returned to Alaska to perform a duty, both as governor and as mother.

On September 11, 2008, in Fairbanks, Sarah Palin gave the keynote address at the deployment ceremony for the Stryker Brigade stationed at Fort Wainwright. The 3,500-soldier brigade was about to be sent to Iraq. It was a regular function of her job, but on this date it had extra significance. One of the members of the brigade was her oldest son, Track.

(Left) Even on the campaign trail there's time for family fun. For Halloween 2008, Trig (held by Willow) is dressed as a baby elephant, and Piper is a snow princess.

VISITOR CENTER
BEAR LODGE

Meeting the Press

That evening, Palin gave her first nationally televised one-on-one interview, with Charles Gibson on ABC's *World News*. The interview drew an estimated 9.7 million viewers, roughly a 25% increase over the program's usual audience. A second portion of the interview was broadcast on *Nightline,* which won its time slot over the late-night talk shows.

One week later, Palin appeared on Fox News' *Hannity & Colmes* show, where she sat for an interview with popular conservative commentator Sean Hannity. The first half of the show focused mainly on the economy, which had recently begun its free fall. The second half, which aired the next day, dealt with national security, Palin's opponents, and the role that her faith plays in her life.

The two interviews weren't enough to sate the public demand for Palin's words. The conventional wisdom was that Gibson, an Ivy League–educated reporter with 40 years of experience, was condescending toward the candidate, while Hannity, whose political leanings were no secret, asked soft questions. It didn't help that there was a perception that the McCain campaign was limiting the media's access to Palin.

Palin's staff decided that Katie Couric of the *CBS Evening News* provided a happy medium. As the anchor of a network news program who had previously interviewed world leaders, Couric had credibility as a journalist. But she, like the governor, was also a working mother of teenagers, and would most likely be sympathetic to her.

In *Going Rogue,* Palin says that she was told it was going to be a short, lightweight interview about balancing a heavy workload with motherhood, with the possibility of a second day of interviewing. Instead, it turned into a series of interviews spread out over several days, with topics ranging from her energy policy to her social views to her reading list.

By her own admission, Palin's performance in her interview with Couric was not her finest hour. She was blindsided and ill prepared for Couric's questions, and she allowed her frustration to show. Palin would also state that her more substantive answers were edited down—or removed entirely—and that the questions where she showed the greatest weaknesses were overemphasized.

(Left) Governor Palin talks with ABC news correspondent Charles Gibson, September 11, 2008.

Intriguing Democrat: Geraldine Ferraro

(Above) Geraldine Ferraro addresses the annual Ultimate Women's Power Lunch for U.S. Representative Jan Schakowsky in Chicago, May 4, 2007. (Right) A congressional report from Representative Geraldine Ferraro's New York district, August 1984.

Congresswoman
Geraldine
FERRARO

NINTH DISTRICT REPORT

Vol. 3, No. 8 — August, 1984

A Guide To Student Financial Aid

Dear Friend:

Whether you are a high school senior considering college next fall, the parent of a student, or perhaps an adult thinking about returning to school, one question everyone has is how to finance a college education. Although the Reagan Administration has severely cut many financial aid programs, there are still funds available. In this newsletter, I offer some suggestions to help you locate available funding.

Throughout your search, you may find it helpful to keep careful records. Use a large calendar to jot down all application deadlines. Make a photocopy of every form and letter you send out. Keep lists of people and organizations you have contacted and follow-up unanswered letters with phone calls.

At times the different qualifications may seem confusing and the red tape frustrating, but the opportunity to begin or continue your education, makes it worth the effort.

I hope this "guide to student financial aid" is useful to you.

Sincerely,

Geraldine A. Ferraro
Member of Congress

FEDERAL PROGRAMS

Eligibility: You must be a U.S. citizen, show financial need, be registered for the draft (unless you are exempt) and you must not be in default of a previous loan.

Forms: Use either of the following forms to apply for federal aid. They are available from your high school counselor or your college financial aid office.

1) The U.S. Department of Education's "Application for Federal Student Aid."
2) The College Scholarship Service's "Financial Aid Form."

FEDERAL GRANTS — do **not** have to be paid back.

Pell Grants—are grants for undergraduate students. Eligibility for the 1984-85 school year is determined by the 1983 financial information you provide on the applica tion. Awards are up to $1,900 based on the level of finan cial need. These grants usually provide the "foundation of aid, to which aid from other federal and non-federa sources may be added. Application deadline: May 1985.

Supplemental Educational Opportunity Grant (SEOG)—are supplemental grants for undergraduate You can receive up to $2,000 a year, depending on yo need, and the availability of SEOG funds at your scho Application deadline: supplied by school.

FEDERALLY ADMINISTERED LOANS — do ha to be paid back.

National Direct Student Loans (NDSL)— NDSL is a low-interest (five percent) loan which m

(continued on pag

(Above) Congresswoman Geraldine Ferraro campaigns with Democratic presidential candidate Walter Mondale before a packed house at the State Capitol of the Minneapolis House of Representatives, St. Paul, Minnesota, July 12, 1984. Mondale chose Ferraro as his vice-presidential running mate against incumbent Ronald Reagan.

Sarah Palin was not the first woman to be the vice-presidential nominee of a major American political party. That honor belonged to Geraldine Ferraro, who was Democrat Walter Mondale's running mate in 1984. The Democrats lost in a landslide to Ronald Reagan, who was reelected to a second term.

Like Palin, Ferraro was not well known beyond her constituency before she was given the nomination. A three-time congresswoman from New York, Ferraro, who was also the first Italian-American on a major party's ticket, faced sexism and considerable scrutiny into her private life.

After the election, she remained active behind the scenes in Democratic politics and has served on the boards of many political and nonprofit organizations. In 1993, President Bill Clinton appointed her to the United Nations Commission on Human Rights, which she later led. Ferraro has twice sought the Democratic nomination for U.S. senator from New York, in 1992 and 1998, but lost during the primaries.

During the 2008 Democratic primaries, Ferraro worked as a surrogate for Hillary Clinton, but she was forced to resign after making racially insensitive remarks about Barack Obama. She eventually endorsed Obama, but was sympathetic to Palin, having seen parallels between the Alaska governor and her own historic run 24 years earlier.

At the time, McCain was running slightly in front of Obama in most polls, with the difference falling within the statistical margin of error. But after Couric's interviews aired, beginning on September 24, Obama began to pull ahead. In the days following the convention, 52% of the country thought Palin was qualified to be president. By early October, that number had dropped to 37%.

There were even some calls in conservative circles for McCain to replace Palin on the ticket, claiming that she lacked the credentials to lead the country should something happened to him. Negative press from liberals was expected, but to hear criticism from the right violated Ronald Reagan's famous "11th commandment," from his 1966 California gubernatorial campaign: "Thou shalt not speak ill of any fellow Republican."

McCain, to his credit, stood beside his running mate, repeatedly stating that she was the best person for the job. On the day the first Couric interview aired, McCain announced that he was suspending his campaign to return to Washington and deal with the nation's financial crisis. Two days later, he resumed his schedule, just in time for his first debate with Senator Obama in Oxford, Mississippi.

(Above) Sean Hannity—conservative television and radio talk-show host, author, and political commentator—interviews Governor Palin on September 17, 2008, in Cleveland.

Governor Palin has coffee with four mothers of active-duty military personnel—Nancy Harding, Julie Devitt, Lee Anthony, and Maureen Snook—in center-city Philadelphia, September 28, 2008. *(in envelope)* Palin's run for the vice presidency reminded some supporters of another reform-minded Republican governor, from the turn of the last century. Also: Among Palin's political heroes is Ronald Reagan, whom she quotes often and cites as an inspiration.

In New York City, Palin examines the NYC Fire Department memorial at Engine Company 10, next to the World Trade Center site in lower Manhattan, September 25, 2008.

Debating Biden

After the Couric fiasco, Palin was given another chance to prove her doubters wrong. When she wasn't giving passionate speeches before huge crowds, she was getting ready for her upcoming debate with the Democratic vice-presidential nominee, Senator Joe Biden of Delaware.

Preparation for the debate began in Philadelphia, but moved to the McCain ranch in Arizona, on Cindy McCain's recommendation, when tensions grew between Palin and the Washington insiders hired as her prep team. The desert sun and fresh air, coupled with the presence of Todd and the kids, calmed things down considerably as they put in long days and the debate drew closer.

On October 2, Sarah Palin and Joe Biden faced off at Washington University in St. Louis, Missouri. Moderated by Gwen Ifill of PBS, the 90-minute debate was watched by 70 million viewers, making it the second-highest-rated political debate in American history.

The candidates stuck to the issues presented in the questions and treated each other cordially and with respect, a far cry from the fiery rhetoric used in their stump speeches. The consensus in the media was that, although Palin performed better than expected, she had failed to deliver the "knockout blow" needed to boost her numbers with undecided voters after the Couric interviews.

(Above) "Can I call you Joe?" The vice-presidential candidates shake hands before the start of their debate at Washington University in St. Louis, Missouri, October 2, 2008. *(in envelope)* A thank-you card autographed by McCain and Palin to a supporter.

In Wasilla, Palin friends and family listen as she debates her Democratic rival, Senator Joe Biden of Delaware. *(Right)* Seattle, Washington, October 2, 2008: tavern-goers at a debate-watching party fill out game cards based on Sarah Palin's comments during her debate with Joe Biden.

"Joe the Plumber" speaks at the Flag Lady's Flag Store in Columbus, Ohio, during the kickoff of his bus tour to campaign for John McCain and Sarah

Intriguing Comic: Tina Fey

When Sarah Palin stepped into the national spotlight, many observers noted her resemblance to Tina Fey, the star of the NBC comedy *30 Rock.* Fey had previously been the head writer and a cast member of NBC's *Saturday Night Live,* which has a long history of lampooning political figures of both parties. It seemed inevitable that she would return to her old stomping grounds to portray the Republican vice-presidential nominee.

When *SNL* began its season on September 13, 2008, the first sketch featured Fey, as Palin, with cast member Amy Poehler as Hillary Clinton, discussing sexism in the election. The sketch was so well received—including by Palin, who called her impression "hilarious" and "spot-on"—that Fey returned two weeks later.

Palin was given her opportunity to rebut Fey's portrayal on October 18, when she made a highly publicized guest appearance on the late-night show. The opening sketch featured Palin, Fey, Alec Baldwin, and *SNL* executive producer Lorne Michaels. She also appeared in the *Weekend Update* news segment with Poehler rapping about Palin.

Fey reprised her impersonation of Palin two more times in the final weeks of the campaign, including a sketch with John and Cindy McCain that aired three days before the election. The comedienne went on to win an Emmy Award for Outstanding Guest Actress in a Comedy Series for her performance.

Following the election, Fey announced that she would no longer play Palin, in order to concentrate on *30 Rock.* But the retirement only lasted 18 months; she brought the character back when she hosted the show on April 10, 2010.

(Right) Tina Fey and Amy Poehler spoof Governor Palin and Senator Hillary Clinton on September 13, 2008.

October 23, 2008: Tina Fey, playing Governor Sarah Palin, is joined by Darrell Hammond as John McCain and Will Ferrell as George W. Bush, on the set of *Saturday Night Live*.

The Homestretch

The poll numbers remained in Obama's favor, but Palin's spirit remained undaunted. If anything, she was even more passionate and devoted to the cause. She took the gloves off, linking Obama to William Ayers, the founder of the Weather Underground, a radical group from the late 1960s and early 1970s.

In the mid-1990s, Obama and Ayers had served together on two nonprofit boards in Chicago, and Obama launched his first campaign for the Illinois State Senate at a fundraiser in Ayers's house. Palin's comments were heavily criticized by liberals, but the governor was simply fighting back after having taken more than her share of personal attacks in the previous five weeks.

McCain and Obama participated in two more debates, with the final one being noted for the frequent mention of "Joe the Plumber." The Holland, Ohio, native, whose full name is Samuel Joseph Wurzelbacher, had earlier had an impromptu conversation with Obama about taxation, which was then broadcast on television and the Internet.

Over the course of the final three weeks of the campaign, the name "Joe the Plumber" became a symbol of the mainstream, blue-collar Americans both candidates were trying to sway. Wurzelbacher became a minor celebrity and appeared with McCain on several campaign stops in Ohio.

Saturday Night Live and Beyond

On October 18, Palin appeared on the NBC sketch-comedy show *Saturday Night Live*. For the past month, much had been made of the governor's resemblance to former cast member Tina Fey, who had impersonated Palin on two previous episodes. Palin would later acknowledge that she once dressed up as Fey for Halloween.

In the opening sketch, Palin was standing in the wings with executive producer Lorne Michaels when actor Alec Baldwin, a frequent *SNL* guest host, walked by. Mistaking Palin for Fey, Baldwin—whose liberal politics are well known—complained to Michaels about having Palin on the show. Michaels corrected Baldwin and introduced him to Palin. Sarah, ever so nicely, got the last laugh by saying that she was a big fan of Baldwin's brother, Stephen, an actor and conservative activist. Palin also appeared in the show's *Weekend Update* news segment.

Alec Baldwin, Sarah Palin, and Lorne Michaels leave 'em laughing in the October 18, 2008, episode of *Saturday Night Live*.

Sarah Palin

In Her Own Words

Hillary Clinton

"I don't agree with all of [Clinton's agenda]. But there are some things that Hillary Clinton did that nobody can take away from her. And that is the 18 million cracks that she put there in that highest and hardest glass ceiling in America's political scene."

—September 17, 2008, Fox News interview on "Hannity & Colmes"

Capitalism

"I am a conservative Republican—a firm believer in free-market capitalism. A free-market system allows all parties to compete, which ensures the best and most competitive project emerges, and ensures a fair, democratic process."

—November 3, 2006, Palin–Parnell campaign booklet, New Energy for Alaska

Special-Needs Children

"One of the great privileges given to me last year was the chance to be a witness for the truth that every child has value; to say to special-needs children that they are beautiful and loved. And needed. We learn more from them than they from us. Across America, a great change is coming in public policy affecting these children, and Alaska can lead the way. This is a part of the culture of life where every child is cherished and protected."

—January 22, 2009, State of the State Address

The U.S. Military

"Let us pay tribute to all our men and women in uniform, and their families, and those who've previously served our great nation. Their fight for freedom allows us to assemble tonight, with liberty and security! Because of their sacrifices we are free to do our jobs here, and we thank them. Todd and our son Track, who is proudly serving in the U.S. Army, thank you [all] for your service."

—January 15, 2008, State of the State Address to the 25th Alaska Legislature

Intriguing Conservative: Joe the Plumber

One of the more intriguing side stories to emerge from the 2008 presidential campaign was the tale of Samuel Joseph Wurzelbacher, a.k.a. "Joe the Plumber." On October 12, Wurzelbacher had a chance encounter with Barack Obama when the Democratic candidate was in his hometown of Holland, Ohio, a suburb of Toledo. Wurzelbacher asked Obama how his small-business tax program would affect his plan to buy the plumbing contracting company he worked for. Obama explained that, although he would get a 50 percent tax credit to pay for his employees' health care, if revenue rose above $250,000, then his taxes would be raised.

A television camera crew following Obama caught the exchange, which was subsequently broadcast on the news. Three days later, at the final presidential debate, John McCain often referred to "Joe the Plumber" as an example of a hard-working American who would be hurt by Obama's economic plan. The nickname caught on, and Wurzelbacher became an instant celebrity and a voice for blue-collar America.

Since the election, Wurzelbacher has been an in-demand presence in right-wing politics. He has spoken at many conservative conferences and Tea Party rallies across the nation. In May 2010, he was elected to the Lucas County Republican Party's central committee.

(Above) Democratic presidential candidate, Senator Barack Obama, is questioned by plumber Joe Wurzelbacher in Holland, Ohio, October 12, 2008. *(Right)* Samuel Joseph Wurzelbacher ("Joe the Plumber") speaks in Elyria, Ohio, with Senator Lindsey Graham and Cindy McCain looking on, October 30, 2008.

Joe the Plumber joins Governor Palin as she speaks at a rally at Bowling Green University in Ohio, October 29, 2008.

Country singer Hank Williams Jr. sings during a rally for Governor Palin at the Missouri statehouse in Jefferson City, November 3, 2008.

JOHN MCCAIN'S CONC
PHOENIX, ARIZONA • N

Thank you. Thank you, my friends.

[cheers, applause]

Thank you for coming here on this beautiful Arizona evening.

[cheers, applause]

My friends, we have—we have come to the end of a long journe
have spoken clearly. A little while ago, I had the honor of calling

[boos]

. . . to congratulate him. . .

[boos]

Please! To congratulate him on being elected the next president
In a contest as long and difficult as this campaign has been, his s
ity and perseverance. But that he managed to do so by inspiring
had once wrongly believed that they had little at stake or little in
something I deeply admire and commend him for achieving.

This is an historic election, and I recognize the special significan
pride that must be theirs tonight.

I've always believed that America offers opportunities to all who
Obama believes that, too. But we both recognize that though we
once stained our nation's reputation and denied some Americans
memory of them still had the power to wound.

A century ago, President Theodore Roosevelt's invitation of Boo
House, was taken as an outrage in many quarters. America today
otry of that time. There is no better evidence of this than the ele
the United States. Let there be no reason now. . .

As the presidential campaign ended its final weeks, Palin crisscrossed the country in her attempts to persuade citizens to vote for her and John McCain. Following a rally in Nevada on November 3, she and her family flew back home to Alaska. Landing in Anchorage the next morning, they drove to Wasilla, where they were greeted by friends and supporters outside City Hall. Then they walked in, cast their votes, and got right back on the plane to go to the McCain reception in Phoenix.

Unfortunately for the Republican ticket, the reception was not as celebratory as they had hoped. At 8:20 in the evening, John McCain conceded the election to Barack Obama with a moving and eloquent speech that noted the significance of the country he had defended electing its first African-American president.

(Above) Palin greets an enthusiastic crowd during a rally in Missouri, November 3, 2008—the day before the big election. *(in envelope)* Senator McCain's concession speech.

Chapter 4

2009 and Beyond

Sarah Palin greets fans on the first stop of her book tour, outside a Barnes & Noble store at Woodland Mall in Grand Rapids, Michigan, November 18, 2009.

Not long after the 2008 presidential election, fans and critics alike began discussing Palin's chances of running for the White House in 2012.

Almost immediately following the McCain/Palin electoral defeat, the fallout from the 2008 presidential election began, as anonymous McCain staffers publicly blamed Palin for the outcome. Sarah returned to Alaska, where she still had a job to do as governor. But the campaign had turned her into a celebrity and thrown Alaska into an unprecedented spotlight.

(Above) February 11, 2009, Juneau, Alaska: Governor Palin answers questions during a news conference, while Director of the Office of Management and Budget Karen Rehfeld looks on. The presidential election is barely three months in the past, and already some critics are accusing her of focusing too much on her national profile and not enough on managing the state.

REP

Palin's family and friends were constantly being bombarded with requests for interviews, and her every public action now was national news. The day-to-day work of running her state mingled with debate about her qualifications to run for president in 2012.

Her approval ratings as governor were still high—around 63%—but nowhere near the numbers of a year earlier. There was starting to be a perception in some circles that Palin cared more about her national ambitions than about the task of running Alaska.

One week after the presidential inauguration of Barack Obama, Palin began to put her newfound status as a conservative hero to good use. She formed SarahPAC, a political-action committee designed to find and support candidates who share her vision and values.

At the same time, a new movement was sprouting across the nation. Many Americans were dissatisfied with the size of the stimulus bill being debated in Congress and the bailing out of corporations in the wake of the economic collapse the year before. Determined to make their voices heard, they began organizing rallies to show their displeasure.

They began calling these events "Tea Parties" after the iconic Boston Tea Party held in 1773, when colonists threw boxes of tea into Boston Harbor to protest taxation without representation. The demonstrations were rooted in the themes that had defined Sarah Palin's career: fiscal conservatism, opposition to big government, and patriotism. The faction found a sympathetic ear at Fox News Channel, whose commentators gave significant coverage to the rallies.

(Preceding page) Governor Palin gives her State of the State address to a joint session of the Alaska Senate and House in the Capitol in Juneau, Alaska, January 22, 2009. In the background, Senate President Gary Stevens and House Speaker Mike Chenault listen.

Sarah **Palin**

IN HER OWN Words

The Death Penalty

"I support adequate funding for a strong public-safety presence in Alaska. Feeling safe in our communities is something we cannot accept any compromise on. This includes policing in all its forms, the court system, prosecutors, and corrections. If the legislature passed a death-penalty law, I would sign it. We have a right to know that someone who rapes and murders a child or kills an innocent person in a drive-by shooting will never be able to do that again."

—*November 7, 2006, Palin–Parnell campaign web site, palinforgovernor.com*

The Right to Bear Arms

"I am a lifetime member of the NRA, I support our Constitutional right to bear arms, and am a proponent of gun-safety programs for Alaska's youth."

—*November 7, 2006, Palin–Parnell campaign web site, palinforgovernor.com*

"We need to send a strong message that law-abiding citizens have a right to own firearms, for personal protection, for hunting, and for any other lawful purpose."

—*February 8, 2008, Alaska Governor's Office press release, "2nd Amendment"*

The Republican Party in Washington

"I believe that Republicans in Washington have got to understand that the people of America are not fully satisfied with all the dealings within the party. Same applies though for the other party, also. Americans are just getting sick and tired of politics as usual, that embracing of the status quo, going with the flow and just assuming that the people of America are not noticing that we have opportunities for good change. We have opportunity for a healthier, safer, more prosperous and energy-independent nation at this time. People are getting tired of a process that's not allowing that progress to be ushered in."

—*September 17, 2008, Fox News interview on "Hannity & Colmes"*

Energy Independence

"We have to consider the need to do all that we can, to allow this nation to become energy independent. It's a nonsensical position that we are in when we have domestic supplies of energy all over this great land. Energy independence is the key to this nation's future—to our economic future—and to our national security."

—*October 2, 2008, vice-presidential debate with Senator Joe Biden*

As the American economy collapsed in 2008, the federal government decided on a two-part solution in order to prevent another Great Depression. The first step was for the government to purchase from banks the bad assets that were at the heart of the problem, for $700 billion. The Emergency Economic Stabilization Act was signed into law by President George W. Bush in October 2008.

Intriguing Conservatives: The Tea Party Movement

The second step was to craft a package that would help stimulate the economy. In February 2009, President Barack Obama signed the American Recovery and Reinvestment Act, through which the government put $787 billion in spending and tax cuts back into the economy.

The bills angered fiscal conservatives, who didn't feel the country could handle adding another $1.5 trillion to an already large debt, especially with so much of it considered to be pork-barrel spending. Despite strong opposition from the right, the stimulus bill passed, and several conservative commentators suggested that citizens should hold rallies to protest the direction the country was taking.

The events were called "tea parties" to draw upon the imagery of one of colonial America's most important events, the Boston Tea Party. On December 16, 1773, colonists in Massachusetts dumped tea into Boston Harbor to protest the British monarchy's taxation of the colony without consent or representation.

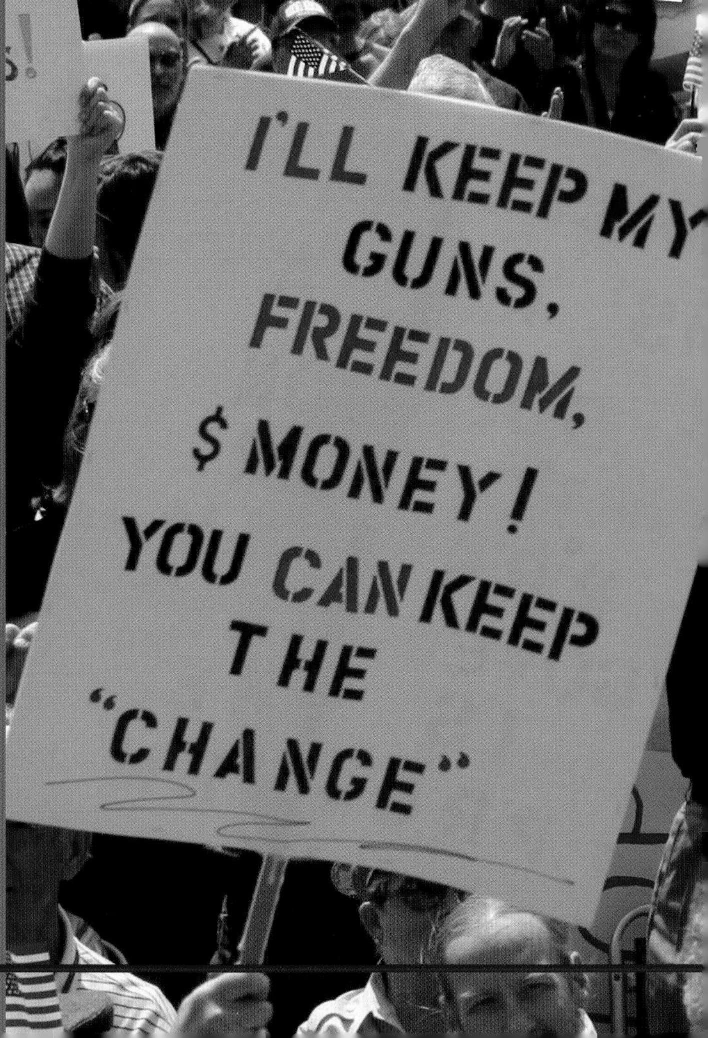

(Above) October 3, 2008, the Oval Office: President George W. Bush signs the Emergency Economic Stabilization Act of 2008—a $700 billion financial bailout bill. Four months later, a government watchdog study would reveal the Bush administration overpaid tens of billions of dollars for stocks and other assets in its massive bailout of Wall Street banks and financial institutions. Such news was fuel for the Tea Party movement.

(Right) April 15, 2010, Salt Lake City, Utah: Tea Party protestors wave "Don't Tread on Me" flags in a tax-reform rally at the State Capitol.

(Right) April 15, 2009, Oklahoma City: about 4,000 people gather on the south steps of the Oklahoma State Capitol—part of a National Tax Day Tea Party—to express their displeasure with government spending.

Sarah Palin waves to fans in front of a road map of the Tea Party Express, before her speech in Boston, April 14, 2010.

News of the public discontent spread, largely due to extensive coverage on the Fox News Channel, and the movement began to get attention in other media as well. It was suggested that like-minded citizens across the nation gather together to hold tea parties on April 15, 2009, colloquially known as Tax Day.

In both big cities and small towns throughout America, people voiced their displeasure with the out-of-control spending. The day was a tremendous success, and the Washington establishment was forced to acknowledge that this was not a "fringe group," as it had been portrayed in some circles.

There were more rallies held on Independence Day, but the Tea Party made its biggest single-event impression in the nation's capital on September 12 with the Taxpayer March on Washington. By then, opposition to President Obama (and especially his proposal to reform the health-care system) had grown. Debate over the health-care plan had raged in highly publicized town-hall meetings all summer long, and the protesters made the controversial package a part of their agenda.

Beginning at Freedom Plaza, hundreds of thousands of protesters dressed in patriotic clothing walked down Pennsylvania Avenue while chanting and carrying signs or flags. The march ended at the U.S. Capitol with a rally whose speakers included several Republican congressmen. The day was part of the 9-12 Project (the brainchild of Glenn Beck of Fox News), which was intended to restore the sense of national unity that immediately followed the terrorist attacks of September 11, 2001.

The Taxpayer March on Washington was also the final stop of the first Tea Party Express, a bus tour that began in Sacramento, California, on August 28 and traveled to 33 cities in two weeks. Its success prompted a second tour, which reached 38 cities in 17 days in October and November.

In January 2010, a special election was held in Massachusetts to fill the U.S. Senate seat vacated by the death of liberal icon Ted Kennedy. The famously Democratic state had not elected a Republican senator since 1972, and that particular seat hadn't been held by a Republican since Kennedy's brother John won it in 1952. Still, conservatives saw this as an opportunity to flex their electoral muscle and break the Democrats' 60-vote "super majority" in the Senate.

Their candidate, state senator Scott Brown, was endorsed by the Tea Party Express, and conservatives from throughout the Northeast campaigned for him. Brown's commercials played up his "average American" credentials, including his hailing from small-town Wrentham and driving a truck. Brown won the seat with 52% of the vote.

(Right) Colonial garb—reminiscent of the original Boston Tea Party and the Revolutionary War—has become a hallmark of the Tea Party movement. Here, a protester at the foot of the Washington Monument has donned a tricorn hat with a tea bag.

Sarah Palin holds up a jersey with her son's name—a gift she received at the Winning Back America conference in Independence, Missouri, May 1, 2010. Palin rallied thousands of Tea Party activists, praising "the people's movement."

The tea parties of 2009 reflected the disenchantment of a growing segment of the public. Although it had high-profile friends at Fox News and similarly minded Washington groups who helped organize many of the events, the movement lacked cohesion. In order to be taken more seriously as a credible voice in American politics, it needed greater organization and structure and a platform to officially determine what it was truly about.

James Bopp, a prominent conservative attorney from Indiana and member of the Republican National Committee, proposed in late 2009 a litmus test to identify potential candidates for office. In order to receive the backing of the RNC, the proposal said, candidates had to agree with at least 8 of its 10 principles. Although the measure was rejected in favor of a nonbinding resolution at the RNC's annual convention in January, the list showed that the tea-party activists were looking to formally define their ideology.

In February 2010, the Tea Party Nation, one of the many groups that sprang up in 2009, held its first convention, in Nashville, Tennessee. The three-day event attracted approximately 600 people, who paid up to $549 to attend, and featured discussions and seminars on how the group could become a more serious and viable force.

The convention gained national attention by hiring Sarah Palin to deliver the keynote address. For her speech, Palin reportedly was paid $100,000, which she donated to conservative causes. Other speakers included former congressman Tom Tancredo and conservative publisher and commentator Andrew Breitbart.

As the 2010 electoral primary season began, the Tea Party began to take on members of the Republican establishment. It was no longer enough to vote the party line, as they believed entrenched politicians had helped to create the current national situation. The popularity of Sarah Palin showed that the movement could best succeed through new faces and fresh ideas.

In May 2010, Bob Bennett, a senator from Utah, lost in his bid for a fourth term when delegates at the state convention nominated two other candidates to challenge for the Republican primary. Although Bennett had an 84% rating from the American Conservative Union, his vote for the bailout bill was seen as a contributing factor to his defeat.

A few days later, Florida governor Charlie Crist, who was seeking the Republican nomination for the Senate, announced that he would run as an Independent. Crist, a moderate who was criticized for embracing President Obama at a public appearance, had fallen more than 20 points behind state House Speaker Marco Rubio in polls leading up to the primary. In the previous year, Rubio, the son of Cuban exiles, had become a fixture at tea-party rallies throughout Florida.

The lack of a third party has long been a point of contention with those, on both the left and right, who have felt that the well-heeled Democrats and Republicans didn't represent their views. The modest successes of the Reform Party in the 1992 and 1996 presidential elections showed that there are large segments of the population who want other options. But whether the Tea Party seeks to become a true third party or becomes folded into the Republican Party, it has already shown that its supporters will demand that their voices be heard.

Palin supporters wait to get their copies of *Going Rogue* signed at Joseph-Beth Booksellers in Norwood, Ohio, November 20, 2009.

Palin's Resignation

Back in Alaska, Sarah Palin was becoming frustrated with a series of ethics investigations that were being launched. By April, there had been 18 investigations into her conduct as governor filed in the span of nine months. Many of the charges came from outside the state, from anonymous sources, or from a well-known critic of Palin's administration.

Although Palin was never formally charged with any wrongdoing, the investigations severely limited her ability to govern the state she loved. As a result of the barrage, her legal bills mounted to over $500,000, and even the establishment of a legal-defense fund led to a complaint (which was eventually dismissed).

On July 3, 2009, as the rest of the country was planning to celebrate Independence Day, Sarah Palin surprised the world again, by resigning as governor of Alaska. In a speech delivered in her backyard overlooking Lake Lucille in Wasilla, Palin began by reminding listeners of her legislative record and how it was accomplished in only two years.

Then she spoke of the ethics complaints and their effect on her administration and her family. Originally, she said, she had decided she would simply not seek a second term. But then she realized that would lead to an 18-month lame-duck session, and she felt that it would be best to leave the job before the completion of her first term. Only by working outside the system of "politics as usual," she said, could she properly fight for Alaska and America.

The resignation took effect on July 26, with Lieutenant Governor Sean Parnell taking control of the state. In her farewell address in Fairbanks, the same city where she was inaugurated, Palin praised our soldiers overseas, reminded Alaska of her record as governor, and asked that the media leave Parnell's kids alone.

(Opposite page) Trustee for Governor Sarah Palin's legal defense fund, Kristan Cole, left, speaks to reporters in Wasilla, Alaska, on July 22, 2009. Cole lashed out at reporters and the Eagle River resident who filed an ethics complaint against Palin.

KRISTAN COLE
FIRST IN
CLOSED TRANSACTIONS
IN ALASKA
Above the Crowd!
TEAM
TOP CLOSED
TRANSACTIONS
2005
TOTAL CLOSED

Sean Parnell was born in California in 1962. When he was 10 years old, he and his family moved to what was then the quiet city of Anchorage, Alaska. The state's oil-and-gas boom soon struck, however; the economy skyrocketed, taking formerly peaceful Anchorage with it. Buildings shot up, roads and parking lots spread, and parts of the city turned into adult playgrounds for oil-field workers with money in their pockets.

Sean's father, Kevin "Pat" Parnell, had grown to love the state of Alaska while at Fort Richardson in 1958 and '59. A printer by trade, and a Democrat with a deep belief in public service, he decided to serve as an assembly member in addition to running his own business. Sean's parents steered a clear and narrow course for their family during those raucous days. Dinner-table conversations focused on the subjects of responsibility, the importance of public service, and theology.

Not mentioned, however, was the fact that Sean's grandfather was a skid-row alcoholic who had verbally and physically abused Pat and his siblings. Pat shielded his children from this information until they were adults. The subject of domestic violence became—and remains—intensely important to Sean. One of his proudest achievements to date is the Domestic Violence Act of 1996.

Pat Parnell, continuing his tradition of public service, began to pursue Alaska's seat in the U.S. House of Representatives. In 1980 he ran as a Democrat against incumbent Don Young but was beaten nearly 3 to 1. He later served a term (1991–1992) in the state House.

Sean, meanwhile, was pursuing his education in the field of law. He met his future wife, Sandy, while working on his Juris Doctorate at the University of Puget Sound. In 1987 he began his own law practice in downtown Anchorage, and he and Sandy married. (They have two daughters, Grace and Rachel.)

Sean was first elected to the state House in 1992. During his two terms, he was a member of the House Finance Committee, chairing several budgetary subcommittees. In 1996 he was elected to the Alaska State Senate, where he was a member of the Energy Council and co-chaired the Finance Committee. He ultimately left the Senate for the private

sector, working in the oil-and-gas business as a lobbyist and in other capacities, before returning to serve the state as deputy director of Alaska's Division of Oil and Gas.

In 2006, Sean was elected lieutenant governor—but he also had an eye on Alaska's seat in the U.S. House of Representatives. Two years later, he announced his intention to challenge Don Young's 18-term hold on that seat. Young's reply was peppery: "Sean," he said, "congratulations. I beat your dad, and I'm going to beat you."

The electoral duel with Young was preempted, however, when Sarah Palin resigned her governorship. It fell to Sean Parnell to serve the remainder of her term, and he was inaugurated governor of Alaska on July 26, 2009. Parnell, known for a quiet, thoughtful, deliberate approach to government, has chosen to run for reelection as governor rather than pursue a seat in the U.S. House of Representatives.

(Opposite) Alaska Governor Sean Parnell, left, shakes hands with Representative Reggie Joule before giving his State of the State address to the Alaska State Legislature in Juneau on Wednesday, January 20, 2010.

(Below) Alaska Supreme Court Justice Daniel Winfee, left, administers the oath of office for governor to Lieutenant Governor Sean Parnell, second left, as Sandy Parnell holds the Bible. Governor Sarah Palin, holding her daughter Piper, and husband Todd Palin watch. The ceremony took place in Fairbanks on Sunday, July 26, 2009.

(Left) Lieutenant Governor Sean Parnell delivers an executive proclamation by Governor Palin during a POW/MIA ceremony on September 19, 2008. The proclamation stated that September 19 would be known as POW/MIA recognition day in Alaska.

Beck addresses the Conservative Political Action Conference (CPAC) in Washington, DC, February 20, 2010.

Intriguing Conservative: Glenn Beck

As a best-selling author and the host of highly rated radio and television shows, Glenn Beck is one of the most influential—and controversial—commentators in the media today. His calls to action and occasionally inflammatory rhetoric against the agenda of the Democratic Party have made him a hero to the right and a lightning rod to the left.

Beck was born on February 10, 1964, one day after The Beatles first appeared on the *Ed Sullivan Show,* and one day before Sarah Palin was born. He began his radio career at the age of 13, when he won a contest with a station in his hometown of Mount Vernon, Washington. A few years later, he was working weekends for a Seattle station. Following his graduation from high school, Beck spent the next 10 years working as a Top 40 "Morning Zoo" disk jockey in many of the nation's largest markets. His outrageous on-air antics and off-color humor often caused controversy, and he rarely lasted longer than a year in any one city.

At the time, Beck had a bad reputation as a hard partier, and he was arrested for drunk driving in Baltimore in the early 1990s. In November 1994, while working in New Haven, Connecticut, he quit drinking and using drugs and began taking his career and life more seriously. His show became more topical, and by 1998 it had moved from Top 40 FM to news-talk AM radio. In 1999, he joined the Church of Jesus Christ of Latter-day Saints.

In 2000, Beck moved to Tampa, Florida, and debuted *The Glenn Beck Program,* which was an instant hit and soon became syndicated across the country. Six years later, while he continued his radio show, CNN's *Headline News* channel hired him to host an evening news program, which ran for two and a half years before he moved to Fox News Channel. The debut of his Fox show coincided with the inauguration of President Barack Obama in January 2009. Beck's first guest was Sarah Palin.

Since moving to Fox, Beck has enjoyed the biggest successes of his career and has had a heavy impact on the direction of the Republican Party. He has been a strong proponent of the Tea Party movement since its origins in early 2009. Beck was also the force behind the "9-12 Project," a platform of 9 principles and 12 values designed to bring back the spirit with which America came together following the attacks of September 11, 2001.

Glenn Beck is also one of the most popular authors in the country, having written six books as of mid-2010, with five of them reaching number one on the *New York Times* bestseller list. Most of his books expand on the values and theories heard daily on his shows. *The Christmas Sweater,* published in 2007, is a fictionalized account of his childhood.

He has taken his talents on the road, performing to sellout crowds across the country in concerts that mix comedy, politics, and motivational speaking.

Beck, who was named one of Barbara Walters's "Top 10 Most Fascinating People of 2009," is married. He and his second wife, Tania, have two children. He also has two children from his previous marriage.

(Above) The U.S. radio-show host, television personality, and best-selling author Glenn Beck, on the "FOX & Friends" cable program, New York, April 20, 2010.

Social-Media Star

Sarah Palin made very few public appearances after she resigned as governor, but she was still able to communicate with her public through her ground-breaking use of the Internet. Her Facebook account allows Palin to go into great detail on matters of importance to her, including criticisms of the Obama administration, publicity about the Tea Party, and candidates she endorses. Her Facebook page has more than 1.5 million fans.

Palin is also active on the social-network site Twitter, which she joined in April 2009. She daily sends out "tweets" to inform more than 125,000 followers on domestic and foreign-policy issues, upcoming appearances and rallies, and worthy causes.

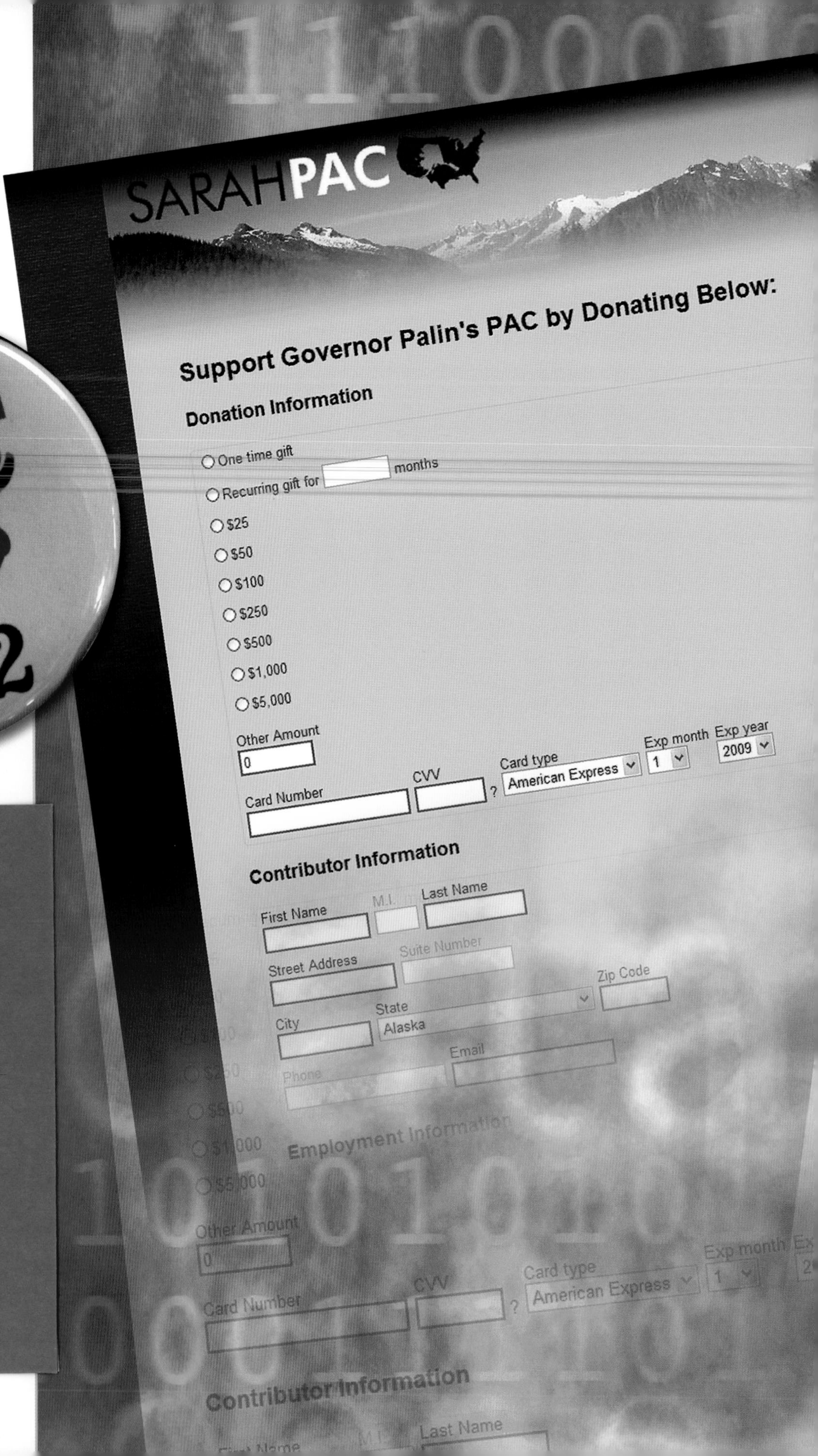

PALIN
2012
facebook
Sarah Palin
Like
Wall
Info
Notes
Donate to S...
YouTube Box
Links
Home
Profile
Account
SARAH PALIN
Going Rogue
An American Life
Suggest to Friends
Sarah Palin + Others
Sarah Palin
Just Others
Sarah Palin
Proud to Support More Women Leaders on the 90th Anniversary of Women's Suffrage Today marks the 90th anniversary of the ratification of the 19th Amendment which granted American women the right to vote...
2 hours ago · View Feedback (4,965) · Share
Sarah Palin I'm traveling with Greta Van Susteren to Alaska's North Slope and ANWR to discuss how developing our resources can contribute to America's energy independence, security, job growth, and economic stability. You'll see what the remote 20 million acres of ANWR with its vast oil and gas reserves really looks like (unlike t...
See More
Monday at 4:27pm · View Feedback (23,522)
Sarah Palin
Legitimate Questions for the President Mr. President, should they or should they not build a mosque steps away from where radical Islamists killed 3000 people? Please tell us your position. We all know that they have the right to do it, but should they? And, no, this is not above your pay grade...
August 14 at 5:34pm · View Feedback (34,202) · Share
Sarah Palin
Alaska's Tough Warrior, Ted Stevens It's with great sadness that Todd and I hear the reports coming in of Senator Ted Stevens' passing in the plane crash near Dillingham. In...
August 10 at 3:37pm · View Feedback (7,948) · Share
Sarah Palin Please remember to vote tomorrow for Bob McConnell to represent Colorado's 3rd Congressional District.
Create an Ad
Facebook Pages
Facebook Pages help you discover new artists, businesses, and brands as well as connect with those you already love.
More Ads
http://www.SarahPAC.com/
http://twitter.com/SarahPalinUSA
2,146,663 People Like This
Donate to SarahPAC
SUPPORT SARAHPAC
SarahPalinUSA
twitter
Get short, timely messages from Sarah Palin
Twitter is a rich source of instantly updated information. It's easy to stay updated on an incredibly wide variety of topics. Join today and follow @SarahPalinUSA.
Sign Up ›
SarahPalinUSA
Proud to Support More Women Leaders on the 90th Anniversary of Women's Suffrage http://is.gd/enDyj
about 2 hours ago via web
Who hijacked term:"feminist"?A cackle of rads who want 2 crucify other women w/whom they disagree on a singular issue; it's ironic (& passé)
about 2 hours ago via Twitter for BlackBerry®
@gretawire Thx for report on America's domestic energy sources! US safety, security &prosperity depend on reliable, economic energy supplies
Now headed to ANWR: 20,000,000 remote acres of US oil & gas;we'll show you what it really looks like,unlike extreme enviro's fundraiser pics
On North Slope w/FOXs Greta VanS..talking ENERGY & America's independence/security/jobs & economic stability;We need to drill;Watch her show
Verified Account
Name Sarah Palin
Location Alaska
Bio Former Governor of Alaska and GOP Vice Presidential Nominee
85 following
224,056 followers
8,871 listed
Tweets 413
Favorites
Following
RSS feed of SarahPalinUSA's tweets
ook.com/sarahpalin

Copies of Sarah Palin's new book, *Going Rogue,* are ready for a book signing at the Costco on December 1, 2009, in Tempe, Arizona. Hundreds of Palin supporters showed up to buy her book and meet the former Alaska governor and 2008 Republican vice-presidential candidate. Just two weeks after publication, the memoir had sold one million copies.

Going Rogue

In November 2009, Palin published her memoir, *Going Rogue: An American Life.* The title refers to a quote by an anonymous McCain staffer, who used the phrase to describe her habit of going off-script, while the subtitle is the name of Ronald Reagan's 1990 autobiography.

The 432-page book tells the story of her remarkable journey from schoolteacher's daughter to governor of Alaska to her resignation. She provides her inside account of what happened during the 2008 campaign. Taking no prisoners, she puts much of the blame on a biased media and on McCain's staff, who tried to micromanage her, although she has nothing but praise for McCain himself. Palin closes the book with her political philosophy, which she describes as "Commonsense Conservative," with its roots in the presidency of her hero, Ronald Reagan.

Going Rogue sold 300,000 copies on the first day of its release, and reached sales of 1,000,000 within the first two weeks. The book was number one on the *New York Times* bestseller list for six consecutive weeks. To promote *Going Rogue,* Palin went on a three-week tour, holding signings in bookstores in mostly small communities in 11 states, and she appeared on Oprah Winfrey's television show. Palin's royalty advance for the book was estimated to be $1.25 million.

In May 2010, she announced that a second book, *America by Heart: Reflections on Family, Faith and Flag,* would be released in November 2010. The book includes many of her favorite readings, including sermons, literature, and poems, and portraits of men and women who reflect her values.

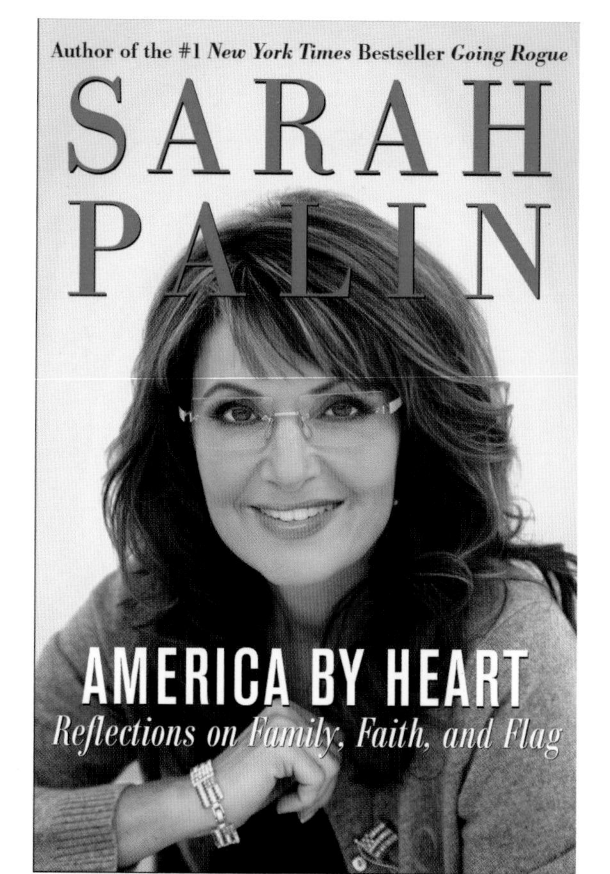

Fans began waiting in line at 5:00 in the morning to get their books autographed at Woodland Mall in Grand Rapids, Michigan, on Wednesday, November 18, 2009—the first stop of Palin's *Going Rogue* book tour.

This signed edition of

Going Rogue

by

SARAH PALIN

has been specially bound by the publisher.

THIS IS NUMBER 3436 OF 5,000 COPIES.

A representative from the 6th district of Minnesota, Michele Bachmann has become one of the most important figures in Republican politics. She is a frequent presence on conservative-leaning talk shows as a fierce critic of the policies of the Obama administration.

Intriguing Conservative: Michele Bachmann

Hailing from Stillwater, Bachmann served six years in the Minnesota state senate before deciding to run for Congress in 2006. Her announcement brought fundraising support from President George W. Bush as well as from religious groups like Focus on the Family.

With her victory, she became the first Republican woman from Minnesota to be elected to the House of Representatives. She currently sits on the Financial Services Committee, which performs oversight of the housing, real estate, and banking industries.

Throughout her time in Congress, Bachmann has reliably spoken out against liberalism and government bailouts for big business. As with Sarah Palin, her conservative social views and willingness to speak her mind have made her a frequent target of the Left.

Bachmann, who was born in 1956, is married and has five children. Her family has also provided foster care for 23 children. She and her husband own a mental-health facility in Stillwater.

(Above) Michele Bachmann regales supporters, including her husband, Marcus (left), at election-night headquarters, November 7, 2006, in Bloomington, Minnesota. She had just won the race for the 6th Congressional District.

(Left) Sarah Palin rallies the crowd after a campaign appearance for Representative Michele Bachmann, April 7, 2010, in Minneapolis.

(Left) The O'Reilly Factor: Conservative talk-show host Bill O'Reilly, pictured here in 2007, hosted Sarah Palin on his program, giving her a chance to speak out on the economy and her critics. *(Above) Real American Stories* focused on the positive: inspiring stories of heroism and generosity that reflected the true spirit of America.

Ready for Her Close-Up

Sarah Palin made the transition from politician to pundit in January 2010, when she joined the team at Fox News Channel. She signed a multi-year deal to contribute to existing shows on the conservative-leaning network and to host a then-undetermined series. The day after the announcement, she appeared on the top-rated *O'Reilly Factor* to discuss President Obama's handling of the economy and to respond to a segment on CBS's *60 Minutes* that was critical of her.

Three months later, she put her broadcast journalism training to further good use when the first installment of her series, *Real American Stories,* debuted on Fox. The show featured inspirational tales of selfless generosity and heroic achievement, with Palin narrating the segments and acting as in-studio host.

In March 2010, Palin signed a deal with cable network TLC to produce an eight-part documentary series entitled *Sarah Palin's Alaska.* The series, produced by Emmy-winning reality-show creator Mark Burnett, is designed to be a tour through the history and natural beauty of the 49th state, as told by its most famous native.

Sarah Palin's Alaska, a project with cable's TLC, was in the making as this book went to press. In this picture, taken in 2008 in Wasilla (when Palin was still governor), the future host of the documentary is interviewed about her trip with the faith-based nonprofit Samaritan's Purse to help deliver aid to villages in Western Alaska.

When Sarah Palin burst onto the national scene in September 2008, people were attracted to more than just her vision for America and her personal story. Her charisma and unique style have also helped her win over millions of people.

Sarah Palin's STYLE

Palin's signature look includes her eyeglasses, the rimless titanium frames by Japanese industrial designer Kazuo Kawasaki. Within two weeks of the Republican National Convention, orders for the glasses, which sell for $375, had quadrupled, according to the brand's U.S. distributor.

Another distinctive feature is her trademark "updo" hairstyle. According to her stylist, Jessica Steele, in Wasilla's Beehive salon, the look came about in 2000 when they were discussing how, as mayor, she needed the public to see her as professional and intelligent.

Palin often wears heels (of varying heights), perhaps to look taller than her 5'5" frame. On the day she was introduced as John McCain's running mate, she caused quite a stir in fashion circles when photographs of the day showed that she was wearing red peep-toe pumps by Naughty Monkey. The brand has been popularized thanks to socialite Paris Hilton, and is often worn by women in their early to mid-20s.

(*Right*) New York City police officers watch as Governor Sarah Palin leaves a hotel in New York, September 24, 2008. Palin and her running mate John McCain just met the presidents of Ukraine and Georgia.

(*Below*) At a campaign rally in Fairfax, Virginia, Sarah Palin stands on stage listening to Senator John McCain, September 10, 2008. Photographers can't resist capturing her shoes and clothes on film.

(Above) Governor Palin listens to questions during an interview in her Juneau office, December 13, 2007.

In *Going Rogue,* the former beauty-pageant contestant defines her no-nonsense look for business as "straight skirts and solid-colored blazers." When in Anchorage, she frequents Second Run, an upscale resale shop, for many of her outfits, and has said that Escada is her favorite label.

For Palin's speech at the convention, the Republican National Committee purchased a white silk Valentino jacket and black skirt with a combined estimated value of $4,000. The outfit, and the other clothes the RNC purchased for her for the campaign, were donated to charity following the election.

Sarah Palin is much more comfortable, however, in casual clothes. In a February 2008 profile in *Vogue* magazine, she joked that her favorite designers were the popular outdoor outfitters Patagonia and The North Face. In *Going Rogue,* she makes several references to wearing Carhartt, whose clothes are built to withstand the rough Alaska weather. She also mentions a preference for Paige Premium jeans, whose founder, former model Paige Adams-Geller, is a native of Palin's hometown of Wasilla.

Just as comfortable in blue jeans: Palin greets supporters at the Asheville Civic Center in North Carolina, October 26, 2008.

(Left) Retired U.S. Air Force Colonel O.P. Ditch wears a shirt supporting former vice-presidential candidate Sarah Palin as he waits in a hallway outside the National Tea Party Convention in Nashville, February 5, 2010. *(Below)* Palin delivers the keynote address at the inaugural National Tea Party Convention—a gathering of about 600 activists from across the country—on Saturday, February 6, 2010.

Leading the Tea Party

Throughout 2009, the Tea Party movement was seen as a grassroots campaign that had plenty of support across the country but lacked the organization and platform needed for credibility. As it gained momentum, its leaders reached out to Sarah Palin to help bring it to the next level.

In February 2010, the Tea Party Nation held its first-ever convention in Nashville, and Palin agreed to deliver the keynote address, on Ronald Reagan's 99th birthday. In her 40-minute speech to a sold-out crowd, she announced that she was a big supporter of the movement and praised its organizers, calling it the "future of politics." She also criticized the Obama administration for wasteful spending and for its handling of foreign affairs, claiming that the president's policies have weakened America.

The speech was followed by a question-and-answer session. Her fee was reported to be $100,000, which she donated to help fund conservative causes.

Palin continued to be an inspirational figure for the movement, and she spoke at a Tea Party rally in March in Senate Majority Leader Harry Reid's hometown of Searchlight, Nevada. On April 15—Tax Day—she addressed a crowd in Boston, the home of the original Tea Party.

In an era of blow-dried, prepackaged politicians offering little more than platitudes, Sarah Palin has reached extraordinary heights by being genuine and unafraid to speak her mind. Her inspiring success is a quintessentially American tale, with her family and faith to keep her grounded. Palin's future endeavors will be praised by her fans and scorned by her detractors. But her appeal and charisma are undeniable, and, whatever she chooses to do next, the world will continue to hang on her every move with great anticipation.

Palin addresses the crowd during the Tea Party rally on the Common in Boston, April 14, 2010.

ABOUT THE AUTHOR

Dave Lifton is a Chicago-based writer whose specialties include modern United States politics, music, and sports. His first exposure to Sarah Palin—like that of most Americans—came in September 2008, when the Alaska governor gave her rallying speech at the Republican National Convention in Saint Paul, Minnesota. Since then he has followed her career on the national scene. In addition to commenting on politics, Lifton manages the Web site *Wings for Wheels* and is also a contributor at *Popdose*. Lifton is the author of *Barack H. Obama: President of the United States, Limited Edition Collector"s Vault,* and was the principal contributor to *Michael Jackson: A Tribute to the King of Pop.* He identifies himself as "a firm believer in the power of new media to establish new voices and tones." He dedicates this book to his mother, whose love and support have been unwavering.

ACKNOWLEDGMENTS

The publisher would like to thank the following individuals and organizations for assisting with this book.

The **Associated Press** provided photographs. Q. David Bowers shared historical postcard images. **Cagle Cartoons, Inc. / PoliticalCartoons.com** provided editorial cartoons. **Miguel Colón Ortiz** fact-checked parts of the manuscript. **Corbis** provided photographs. **Ronald Devito** shared personal memorabilia. **Jill Dible** shared personal memorabilia. **Getty Images** provided photographs. **Heritage Auction Galleries** provided photographs. **Deb Murphy** provided image research. The **National Archives** provided certain historical images. **Liz Pavek** contributed an essay. **RR Auctions** shared imagery of historical memorabilia.

Various coin photographs are from *A Guide Book of United States Coins,* 64th edition (Yeoman).

Associated Press Photographs

26, 66; File, 67
ABC, Donna Svennevik, 88
Abrams, Henny Ray, 94, 136
Alaska Governor's Office, Christopher T. Grammer, 62
Alaska Tourism Council–John Hyde, 12
Altaffer, Mary, File74
Anchorage Daily News, Bill Roth, 12
Anchorage Daily News, Erik Hill, 45
Anchorage Daily News, Evan R. Steinhauser, 36
Applewhite, J. Scott, 59; File, 95
Arbogast, Charles Rex, 75, 90
Beckham, Fred, 84
Broome, Gerry, 34
Christensen, Jeff, 134
Cole, Jim, 55
Daily Sitka Sentinel, James Poulson, 12
Daly, Matthew, 122
Department of Defense, 63
Department of Defense, Pvt. Christopher T. Grammer, 61
Department of Defense, Sgt. Jacob A. McDonald, 61
Dharapak, Charles, 69, 116
Drew, Richard, 127
Edelson, Dana / NBCU Photo Bank via AP Images, 98, 100
Edmonds, Ron, 77, 83
Fox News Channel, 92
Franklin, Ross D., 130
Gaps III, John, File19
The Grand Rapids Press, Rex Larsen, 108, 131
Grillo, Al, 8, 11, 13, 20, 21, 22, 26, 33, 37, 39, 42, 43, 46, 48, 49, 52, 54, 56, 57, 58, 80, 82, 96, 112, 125, 135; File, 29, 44, 56, 64
Hage, Matt, 21
HALEY/SIPA, 119
Helber, Steve, 58
Heller, John, 86
Herbert, Gerald, 85
Herbert, Gerald, 137
Hong, Jae C., 104
IDW Publishing, 68
The Independence Star, Susan Pfannmuller, 120
Kaczmarek, Joseph, 93
Kaster, Carolyn, 68
King, Andy, 28
Klein, Robert E., 140
Krupa, Charles, 118
Lieberman, Dr. Scott M., 92
Magana, Jose Luis, 126
Mat-Su Valley Frontiersman, 23, 32
Mihalek, Tom, 35, 55
Miller, Chris, 53, 56, 124; File, 60, 111, 138
Mone, Jim, 133
Neibergall, Charlie, 75, 78, 79
Ogrocki, Sue, 117
Osorio, Carlos, 110
Payne, Wade, File, 138
Redmond, Nell, 141
Reinke, Ed, File, 142
Riedel, Charlie, 106, 107
The Salt Lake Tribune, Scott Sommerdorf, 117
Salzman, Larry, 91
Sancetta, Amy, 105
Sancya, Paul, 70
Sato, Kiichiro, 72, 97
Savoia, Stephan, 61, 65, 76, 137, 139
Schultz, Rich, 141
Sheakley, David J., 57
Tesfaye, Bizuayehu, 143
Thompson, Elaine, 97
U.S. Fish and Wildlife Service, File, , 20
Uhlman, Tom, 121

Getty Images Photographs

Michael Sugre / Contour by Getty Images
Brian Adams / Contour by Getty Images

Cartoons

© 2008 Randy Bish / Political Cartoons, 74, 135
© 2008 Daryl Cagle / Political Cartoons, 87
© 2008 John Cole / Political Cartoons, 72
© 2008 Mike Keefe / Political Cartoons, 43
© 2009 Mike Lane / Political Cartoons, 123
© 2008 R.J. Matson / Political Cartoons, 64
© 2008 Petar Pismestrovic / Political Cartoons, 67

Corbis Images Photographs

Marcus, Steve / Reuters / Corbis, 30, 50, 102, 114

Government Organizations

Biographical Directory of the United States Congress, 40, 41
Executive Office of the President of the United States, 19, 93
Library of Congress, 10, 18, 19, 24, 25, 27, 50, 93
Library of Congress / Marion S. Trikosko, 102
National Archives, 15, 17
Office of Congresswoman Michele Bachmann, 132
Office of United States Senator Ted Stevens, 40
U.S. Air Force photo/SSgt Joshua Garcia, 125
U.S. Air Force photo / TSgt Scott Seyer, 41
United States Senate official photo, 84
White House Photo Office, 142

Istockphoto.com

Bergmann, Dean, *inside front cover*
brytta, 10
Canning, Ken, 20, *inside front cover*
lightasafeather, *inside front cover*
Tessier, Paul, *inside front cover*
toddmedia, 10

Other Photos

George, Angela, 38
Kovalchek, Frank, 27
Kozaryn, Linda D., 38
Margaret Thatcher Foundation, 142
McPhee, Nic, 25
Proudfoot, Rona, 104
Ramsey, Derek and Julie, 27
Shankbone, David, 99
Teterenko, James, 35